ENCOU

ENCOUNTERS

Jesus, connection and story:
past, present and future

RACHEL TREWEEK
Bishop of Gloucester

DARTON·LONGMAN+TODD

First published in Great Britain in 2020 by
Darton, Longman and Todd Ltd
1 Spencer Court
140–142 Wandsworth High Street
London SW18 4JJ

Print book ISBN: 978-0-232-53466-5
Ebook ISBN: 978-0-232-53467-2

A catalogue record for this book is available from the British Library.

Designed and produced by Judy Linard
Printed and bound in Great Britain by Bell & Bain Ltd, Glasgow

This book is dedicated with thanksgiving
to my family and friends and all the
companions I have encountered on the way.

Most particularly I give thanks for Guy whose
love and kindness knows no bounds.

CONTENTS

FOREWORD *by Justin Welby, Archbishop of Canterbury* 9

PREFACE 13

INTRODUCTION 17

Chapter 1 THE 'YES' OF THE HEART 25

Chapter 2 THE SEEING OF THE HEART 34

Chapter 3 THE WET FOOTPRINTS OF OUR BAPTISM 42

Chapter 4 TASTING THE KINGDOM OF GOD 51

Chapter 5 PLACE AND NAME 60

Chapter 6 SHARING THE STORY 68

Chapter 7 BELOVED DAUGHTERS 77

Chapter 8 IDENTITY 87

Chapter 9 THE RHYTHM OF GOD 96

Chapter 10 INSIDE OUT 104

Chapter 11 IF ONLY 113

Chapter 12 FEET AND HEART 121

Chapter 13 EXPLORING THE DARK 130

Chapter 14 THE GARDEN OF ENCOUNTER 139

Chapter 15 THE ROAD TO EMMAUS 147

ACKNOWLEDGEMENTS 157

FOREWORD

by Justin Welby,
Archbishop of Canterbury

It feels somewhat ironic to be writing this foreword to Bishop Rachel's book about 'encounter' at a time when for so many of us our experience of encounter with one another has changed so drastically due to the outbreak of Coronavirus. We no longer go to meet our friends, see our colleagues every day, or even gather together in our churches on a Sunday. Encounter and relationship as we know it seems to have changed greatly in such a short period of time.

And yet there could be no better moment for Bishop Rachel's book, which reminds us that the tangle and connectedness of human lives cannot be broken, and God's relationship with us knows no limits or barriers. We have learnt at this time of the great interconnectedness of all humanity and our utmost dependence on God.

In the Bible, we see time and time again that people are deeply changed by their encounters with Jesus Christ. They are healed and accepted, seen and loved. They begin to live a new life, a resurrection life, when they turn to Jesus amongst the brokenness of the world and have faith in him. Many of the characters who meet Jesus in scripture are very human, with faults and flaws just as you and I have, and yet something about meeting Christ transforms them. It gives them permission to live in the knowledge that they are known, loved and welcomed by God.

The presence of Jesus Christ has sustained and changed the lives of billions of people in the subsequent millennia – his enduring relationship with us continues and draws us together as one family, coming together from around the globe. Christians depend on this relationship, on their encounter with the risen Christ, even though we cannot necessarily see him as his first disciples did. At this time, when many of the ways we would normally maintain our relationship with Jesus and our fellow brothers and sisters in Christ are unavailable to us in the normal ways, we are reminded of the glorious news that we can always deepen our personal relationship with Christ and encounter him through prayer. We delight in the fact that our relationship with our fellow Christians endures and continues as we maintain our fellowship in difficult times, just as the earliest Christians did.

As we face our current challenges, and think about how we can bring our world just that bit closer to the kingdom of heaven, Bishop Rachel has, as ever, been prescient in identifying that it is through relationship and connection that we can participate in God's mysterious but wonderful work here on earth.

This book is also a story of Rachel's life, and her own relationship with Christ. Just like those many characters in the Bible, her faith in Jesus has transformed her journey, leading her on adventures she could never have imagined. Her life fulfils what she has learnt from her faith – to lay aside preconceptions, to be passionate in your callings, and to trust in the Lord and follow where he calls you, even if you are not always so sure yourself! She is a testament to the fact that if you invite Jesus into your life, he will be there every step of the way, throughout the tribulations as well as the triumphs.

This book is but one more gift with which Bishop Rachel has blessed the church. Her selfless service has in turn transformed countless other lives and shown many the value and joy of being loved by God. Her hope, her love of others and her passion for Jesus shines through on every page. I hope that you find her writing, as I have, inspiring, enriching and uplifting. Even in these toughest of times, we can encounter Christ anew as he holds out his arms in loving welcome, inviting us into a relationship with him that will last forever.

Justin Welby
Archbishop of Canterbury
May 2020

PREFACE

I began this book in the summer of 2019 and all except the last chapter was completed later that year and in the early days of 2020. Never did I imagine that its publication would be delayed due to a world-wide viral pandemic.

A period of so-called lockdown began towards the end of March 2020 and people were largely confined to their homes. Public buildings stood closed including places of worship. A gradual and phased emerging from lockdown did not begin for nearly three months, with continually evolving government guidance regarding the limits on people's freedom and the size and nature of various gatherings. In all of this a few things have remained constant including the requirement to adhere to what has been termed 'social distancing' – the need to keep physical distance from those who are not members of the same household.

I don't know who first invented the term 'social distancing' but from the outset I have refused to use it, preferring the words 'physical distancing' as this more accurately describes what is required. For me the words 'social distancing' express something which is already far too prevalent in our country and world and indeed describes much of what Jesus Christ stands against in the gospel narratives as he intentionally moves towards those who are socially othered and marginalised by those around them, including the religious leaders of the day.

This book with its focus on encounter seeks to celebrate everything that the term social distancing does not. It is about community and intimacy and the discovery of self in close encounter with God and neighbour.

The impact of COVID-19 has been devastating in so many

ways as people have experienced loss so frequently centred on relationship. People have not only experienced bereavement due to the death of loved ones, but also the loss of meeting face-to-face with friends and family, and the absence of interaction with people in the routines of everyday life. Many people of all ages and backgrounds experienced increased isolation and a diminished sense of well-being as places of encounter ranging from the school playground to clubs and groups were suddenly removed from daily life or only available in a virtual world through the use of technology.

Yet it is also true that amid the fear and devastation many good news stories have emerged and these too have had relationship at the heart. There are numerous stories of neighbourly kindness, community projects including food provision, individual phone calls, messages of care and umpteen stories of connection made across digital platforms as people have gone towards one another in relationship – the opposite to being socially distanced.

In aiming to navigate well the uncharted waters ahead, still so full of uncertainty, the headline words highlighted in my introduction seem apposite. In both the storm and the calm, whether within or around, I need to pay attention to *relationship* and *connection*, and perhaps now more than ever there is a need to embrace that spirit of *adventure* with Jesus Christ, through both the tears and the laughter.

When I was in Tiberias in 2019 I saw how frequently the evening winds whip up the waves on the Sea of Galilee. Being in a boat on turbulent waters would not have been unfamiliar to Jesus' disciples but that didn't mean that their anxiety was any the less acute each time they experienced it. More surprising to me is their lack of expectation regarding Jesus.

Even after they have experienced something of Jesus' miraculous work and participated in the feeding of five thousand people with one tiny picnic, the disciples are still terrified as they see Jesus walking towards them on the stormy water (John 6:16-21). Then in each of the gospel accounts of this episode we hear Jesus speak the words 'It is I; do not be afraid', and there is a strong resonance with the words God spoke to Moses hundreds of years before in a mysterious encounter by a burning bush when God described himself as 'I am' (Exodus 3:14). The one who walks towards his disciples on the choppy waters is mysteriously and inextricably connected to the one who created the sea.

I am acutely aware that whereas so much of the activity of human encounter is severely changed during a time of viral pandemic, the God of relationship is unchanged and I am reminded to stay expectant and to allow my imagination and heart to be enlarged in a willingness to embrace fresh discovery and deeper mystery. As with the disciples, there is a strong desire for Jesus Christ to be in the boat with us and to stay close, however distant the shore.

August 2020

INTRODUCTION

In March 2015 it was announced that I was to be the next Bishop of Gloucester and from that day on life has been a continuous succession of waves, with one following on from another in fairly rapid succession. It was therefore a great gift to live ten weeks of sabbatical during the summer of 2019 as I marked the fourth anniversary of my consecration. Those ten weeks were a time for rest and reflection as well as connection and reconnection.

I am deeply aware that I have been significantly shaped by my experiences and encounters with people and places both past and present. Encounter that has sometimes been joyous and sometimes painful. Encounter that has sometimes been life-giving and sometimes life-diminishing. Encounter that has sometimes involved beginning and endings. And at the heart of it has been the heart of God who calls me by name and goes on calling me as I seek to follow Christ in the power of the Holy Spirit.

I decided therefore to take 'Encounter' as my sabbatical theme and to spend time reflecting on Jesus Christ's encounters as presented in the Gospels, alongside days spent with a few people and places from my past years. This ranged from time with individual friends and family to some days in South Africa where I did a placement in 1994, just prior to the first democratic elections.

Relationship, connection and flourishing

At the heart of encounter is our three-in-one God of relationship and the truth that in love we are created in God's image to live in relationship with God, each other and the created world.

Relationship and *connectedness* have become big words within me and it is only more recently as I have looked back on my life that I have better understood my first calling to be a paediatric speech and language therapist.

My years of clinical practice were about communication, connection and enabling children, families and communities to relate to one another. My work reflected what was at that time, an unspoken commitment to flourishing and human potential, whatever labels of disability and deprivation were assigned to children and adults.

Perhaps unsurprisingly my therapeutic work with children and families led me into the sphere of family therapy with its focus on human systems and connections, although my professional training as a family therapist was thwarted by a call to ordination which came as an unwanted interruption. However, I soon came to realise how relevant it is to look at worshipping communities and their contexts through the various lenses of family therapy.

I completed my study for a Diploma in Couples and Family Therapy during my curacy, recognising that so many of the concepts in family therapy resonate with Christian theology not only regarding interdependence and the metaphor of the body of Christ, but also with the clear trajectory in Scripture of our connection with the past and future. However, at the time of my study I was viewed as an unusual course member and I remember being encouraged by one of my tutors at the Institute for Family Therapy to write about my insights. Sadly it did not seem to be something I could prioritise at that time, but in more recent years I have sometimes felt disappointed that I did not commit my thoughts to the printed page as so much learning from family therapy has now emerged as influential within the field of Christian pastoral studies, conflict resolution and church leadership (although my disappointment probably says more about my pride).

A further area of my ministry which is undoubtedly rooted in a focus on relationship and connection is that of conflict transformation. Over the years I have not only enjoyed furthering my personal learning and training but have also relished opportunities in the Church to lead training sessions, workshops and discussions where I have used insights from both family therapy and conflict resolution. It also shaped much of my work in my years as an Archdeacon.

As I stand in the present, looking back to the past and continue to go on becoming, I know that relationship, connectedness and reconciliation have been and always will be at the core of my life and ministry, not least as I go on discovering more of both my beauty and my brokenness, and what I need to go on receiving as well as discovering more of what I have to give.

Imagination

During my sabbatical I spent two weeks in Tiberias on the shore of the Sea of Galilee. This time was primarily about focusing on Jesus' encounters in the Gospels and it was during prayer, reflection and imagining that this book began to take form.

My imagination was also being stimulated as I immersed myself in ten novels, each of which had been recommended by a member of the Diocese of Gloucester senior staff team. As I read each book, I enjoyed ruminating on what it was about each novel that had made it a personal favourite for each colleague. Not only was this about 'connection', but it also resonated with my treasuring of story and imagination.

As a child I loved both reading and writing stories, and my response to that question often asked by adults, 'What do you want to be when you grow up?' was that I wanted to be 'an author of children's books'. It amuses me now that when I wrote that in pencil at the age of seven, my class teacher crossed out 'author' and wrote 'authoress' next to it as a spelling correction. Perhaps even at that young age, alongside a delight in relationship and connection expressed through the characters and place of story, I was also subconsciously expressing a commitment to gender equality!

Over the years I have grown to value my imagination as a God-given gift, whilst being very aware that at some point in life the flames of imagination, fanned in children, are often quenched and given less attention unless they stimulate the intellect or are economically productive.

When I was introduced to Ignatian spirituality in my twenties it was so freeing to hear the imagination being commended. It was as if part of me that had been secreted away gradually began to emerge to once more take a celebrated place in my life. My encounters with God were enriched as I acknowledged the sacred space of my imagination as it was awoken.

The adventure of the Kingdom of God

When I think back to the books and stories I most enjoyed as a child not only were adventure, mystery and relationship common themes but also the 'otherness' of kingdoms unseen. Whether it was the world of C. S. Lewis's Narnia or Tolkien's Middle Earth or Sleigh's Kingdom of Carbonel I found these mythical 'other worlds' tantalising and exciting.

While some might say that my adult faith is simply a further indulgence in the world of fairy-tale and make believe I would respond with those words of *encounter* and *relationship* writ large. My encounter with the hope and love of Christ within a living relationship is no fantasy, and this is not about 'another world' but rather it is about the mystery of this present creation being made new. As Tom Wright puts it '"God's kingdom" in the preaching of Jesus refers not to post-mortem destiny, not to our escape from this world into another one, but to God's sovereign rule coming "on earth as it is in heaven".'[1] If you asked me in the present not that question from childhood about what I want to be when I grow up but instead a question about my calling now, my response would be about 'being' and would include the big words of *hope* and *flourishing* and I would express something about participating in the Kingdom of God coming on earth as in heaven and God's mysterious work of love, reconciliation and transformation, and always in relationship:

[1] N. T. Wright, *Surprised by Hope: Rethinking Heaven, the Resurrection, and the Mission of the Church*. (SPCK, 2011)

Then I saw a new heaven and a new earth; for the first heaven and the first earth had passed away, and the sea was no more. And I saw the holy city, the New Jerusalem, coming down out of heaven from God, prepared as a bride adorned for her husband. And I heard a loud voice from the throne saying,

'See, the home of God is among mortals.
He will dwell with them; they will be his peoples,
and God himself will be with them;
he will wipe every tear from their eyes.
Death will be no more;
mourning and crying and pain will be no more,
for the first things have passed away.'

And the one who was seated on the throne said, 'See, I am making all things new.' Also he said, 'Write this, for these words are trustworthy and true.' (Revelation 21:1-5)

I hold fast to God's promise of 'shalom' – that one day there will be no more tears, no more pain, no more dying and that relationship with God and all creation will be fully restored, yet in the present the vision and commitment to flourishing and justice and reconciliation is often tough going and the key is as frequently in the minor as the major.

Some days the vision of hope and justice can seem shrouded in a dark mist amid pain and struggle, both personal and that of the world. I feebly grope around to keep it in sight and strain to reach out and touch it, and yet I know that as I participate in creation's groaning this is still the stuff of adventure.

In reality, adventures frequently involve loss, pain, fear, unexpected tragedy, tears, disappointment and struggle before there is resolution. The invitation to participate in the adventure of the Kingdom of God is an invitation to human being and human becoming, and saying yes requires me to embrace the truth that crucifixion and resurrection dwell together as I go on becoming the person God created me to be.

21

Yet the more I discover, the more the mystery grows and the larger the emerging question marks. Perhaps I am beginning to learn more of what it means to become once more like a little child, for when Jesus put a child in the midst of the disciples and said 'unless you change and become like children, you will never enter the kingdom of heaven',[2] I believe he was underlining the need for imagination, curiosity and honest questioning rather than erudite answers.

Silence, discovery and mystery

Hand-in-hand with my treasuring of the God-given gift of human imagination goes my love of silence. And by that I mean not the silence of loneliness or denial but rather that which creates solitude and the space for discovery of God and self, and that interconnectedness of humanity and the world around. A discovery which is rarely about answers but is rather about being drawn into the ever greater mystery of God who is so totally other and yet intimately close (what is theologically termed as God's transcendence and immanence). I was therefore very grateful during my sabbatical for an abundance of silence, and in the writing of this book I found myself returning again and again to the discoveries made during my retreat in Massingham in Norfolk in 1998 as I lived the Spiritual Exercises of St Ignatius Loyola. I spent thirty days in silence except for a short meeting every evening with my spiritual director. My days were shaped by prayer, contemplation of scripture and reflection. Externally life was stress-free, with no responsibilities or engagement with other people. Internally it was exhausting as I could not easily be distracted from my inner landscape or encounter with God. During my weeks of sabbatical I returned to my journal from that life-changing retreat and it has elicited fresh places of curiosity within me.

I have become ever more aware of how my landscape of relationship and connection is woven through with a

[2]   Matthew 18:3.

commitment to story and imagination and imbued by an ever-growing sense of life's mystery and adventure as God's kingdom continues to break in.

The shape of this book

In the pages that follow I have endeavoured to share some of my thoughts which have coalesced around different themes as I have spent time with some of Jesus Christ's encounters in the gospels from his being in the womb of his mother Mary before his earthly birth, through to his encounters on the day of his earthly resurrection. Those gospel narratives have led to these pages of fairly random personal reflections on some of the people and places that have shaped me, as well as my thoughts on different issues and a few of the discoveries I have made in my ongoing mysterious adventure with God.

Each chapter begins with a gospel encounter and ends with a prayer or song from a different source. It is my hope that as you read this book it might enable you to make new discoveries and connections in your own adventure with the God of relationship, so there is a blank page at the end of every chapter for you to draw or jot down your own thoughts.

I close these pages of introduction with an experience on the fourth anniversary of my consecration on the feast of Saint Mary Magdalene. My husband Guy and I chose to spend time in Magdala where a site is still being developed following the archaeological discovery a few years ago of the first-century city.

It was very special to spend time in the modern church (Duc In Altum) which has a number of side chapels with colourful mosaics portraying gospel encounters between Jesus and various people, including Mary Magdalene. Towards the end of our time there I went downstairs and entered the chapel which has a floor from the first-century market place in the port at Magdala where it is highly likely that Jesus once walked. My eyes were immediately drawn to an enormous modern painting by a Chilean artist, Daniel Cariola, of ankles and sandaled feet. Those of Jesus are at the centre and there is an outstretched arm of a woman with her index finger just touching the hem of Jesus' robe. A circle of light depicts the power going out of Jesus into the woman as her healing takes place. It is of course capturing the narrative of the haemorrhaging woman as told in Mark 5:25-29, and in an instant I experienced this chapel as a place where heaven and earth embraced.

A little later the priest told me that the chapel had been named 'Encounter'. I gasped audibly as this was the title of my sabbatical and here on the anniversary of my consecration I had experienced a place of connection with God which had mysteriously renewed me in my calling as I reached out to Christ and knew the strength of his 'yes'.

Chapter 1

THE 'YES' OF THE HEART

In the sixth month the angel Gabriel was sent by God to a town in Galilee called Nazareth, to a virgin engaged to a man whose name was Joseph, of the house of David. The virgin's name was Mary. And he came to her and said, 'Greetings, favoured one! The Lord is with you.' But she was much perplexed by his words and pondered what sort of greeting this might be. The angel said to her, 'Do not be afraid, Mary, for you have found favour with God. And now, you will conceive in your womb and bear a son, and you will name him Jesus. He will be great, and will be called the Son of the Most High, and the Lord God will give to him the throne of his ancestor David. He will reign over the house of Jacob for ever, and of his kingdom there will be no end.' Mary said to the angel, 'How can this be, since I am a virgin?' The angel said to her, 'The Holy Spirit will come upon you, and the power of the Most High will overshadow you; therefore the child to be born will be holy; he will be called Son of God. ... Then Mary said, 'Here am I, the servant of the Lord; let it be with me according to your word.' (Luke 1:26 – 38)

On first reading, this might not be viewed as one of the gospel encounters with Jesus, yet it could be seen as the threshold of Jesus' first earthly encounter with another person – his mother Mary.

Mary's encounter with the Angel Gabriel has inspired

paintings, Christmas cards and stained glass windows and every year there are numerous nativity plays in schools and church buildings involving little girls dressed in blue, clutching a plastic doll.

We know the story, and in the midst of flux in our lives we can find the predictability of the story and the recurring annual Christmas traditions deeply reassuring. Yet the irony is that Mary's story of saying yes to God is an invitation to let go of the known and the deceptive security of the familiar and to learn more about what it means to be truly dependent on God.

Here is a young unmarried woman preparing for marriage, living in an unremarkable place and no doubt living with her own internal longings, hopes and fears. Into this very ordinary, seemingly very unremarkable life comes a shocking visit from an angel as Mary-from-nowhere is told that she has been chosen to carry God's child – to give birth to God's son – the long-awaited Messiah.

In the scene of Mary's encounter with the Angel Gabriel there is a need to 'let go' of all prepossessed ideas and judgements and to acknowledge that God's way of coming to earth defies all expectations. Mary says 'yes' in the words that have come to be known as the Magnificat.[3]

Mary sings with joy that God has looked with favour on the lowliness of God's servant and I am challenged to recognise that I am on dangerous territory, not only when my pride and arrogance are the drivers for shaping my activity, but also when they define the territory of my faith and my relationship with God.

The invitation to 'let go' pervades Mary's story. Towards the end of Mary's unexpected pregnancy comes an arduous journey to Bethlehem for a huge exercise in bureaucracy. If the journey wasn't bad enough in itself, Mary then goes into labour in a strange place as she and Joseph find themselves alongside animals, miles from home. I wonder what was

[3] Luke 1:46 – 55

going through her head as she experienced the pain of labour in rather uninviting circumstances.

We have grown so accustomed to the story so that as we watch children with heads adorned with tea towels and tinsel act out a touching story we love and know so well, we are rarely challenged or shocked by the way God chose to bring the Messiah, Wonderful Counsellor and Prince of Peace into the world.

I'm ashamed to say that sometimes my tiny mind and proud heart are full of big preconceived ideas and I have become deaf to the reality of Mary's song that God has scattered the proud in the imagination of their hearts. God has scattered the proud with all their plans and will go on doing so. And I am slow to learn.

As a teenager I developed the ambition to become a speech and language therapist. I had talked about possibly becoming a teacher or perhaps doing something medical, and somehow through various conversations a seed was planted in my mind. I went to observe a local speech and language therapist and did not look back in the decision about my career path.

So it was that I spent four years at the University of Reading studying Linguistics and Language Pathology. I moved to London and took up my first post as a paediatric speech and language therapist based in a rather rundown health centre in the middle of an estate in Gospel Oak.

Looking back, the story of that appointment did involve a letting go, albeit a reluctant one. In many ways I had no desire to move to London; I viewed it as a rather frightening place, but during my training I had met an amazing therapist and manager of speech therapy services across three London health authorities. Her name was Dr Lena Rustin, and she pulled no punches. In my student years she led a number of training sessions focused on management and self-awareness. As students we found her direct approach and the challenges she set us somewhat daunting and her personal judgements were often harsh. The iron fist did not come wrapped in velvet. However, I admired her leadership and insights and knew that working under her would stretch me and equip me for the future. Therefore, when a vacant post arose in her area at an appropriate level for a new graduate, I applied. My excitement at being called for interview was short lived as the appointment day was set for a date when I was to be on holiday in Switzerland. There was no flexibility and Lena was clear that if I wanted to be on holiday then I had to forego any possibility of acquiring the job. I was bitterly disappointed and still clearly remember the group walk in Switzerland on the day of the interview. It involved a heavy heart and a silent letting go through clenched teeth.

On the day of my return to England there was a letter awaiting me inviting me to an interview for the exact same post. There had apparently been something amiss regarding the successful candidate at the first round of interviews and the offer had been withdrawn. So it was that I was interviewed and subsequently appointed.

Thus began seven years as a speech and language therapist in health centres, nurseries, homes and schools. Those years included a post as part of a new Child Development Team attached to the Royal Free Hospital, plus two years as a clinical manager of paediatric therapists. During those years I became exposed to family therapy and systemic thinking and felt a strong pull to explore this path alongside my communications work. It seemed to be part of the next season of my calling, and so I was somewhat confused when a strong call towards ordination began to well within me.

During this time I had become involved with All Souls Clubhouse, a local worshipping community in London's West End immersed in the life of the wider community under the leadership of Simon Parke. Although at the beginning it was not always a place where I felt at ease, my soul began to sing in new ways as relationships deepened with a wide variety of local people of different ages, many carrying painful chapters in their story. I was given opportunities for leading groups and worship and I discovered a whole new area of spirituality in which the mystery of God became more apparent. Yet, with all this discovery came an unwelcome pull to explore full-time ministry. I consoled myself with the belief that it was all about many years hence and not for the present, but when I finally succumbed to meet with Simon to share my thinking he simply looked at me and said something along the lines of, 'I have been waiting for you to say that.' He asked me lots of pertinent questions and I certainly did not leave the room singing anything vaguely like Mary's words. Instead I began to wrestle and tried to negotiate with God. This all came to a climax one particular night after a production of the annual Clubhouse pantomime. (Incidentally, in writing this book I have found it interesting to note how often pantomimes seem to feature in the story of my adventure with God.)

This particular night I lay in bed tossing and turning, attempting to argue with God that my work with families, schools, community groups and related professionals was of far more use to God than what I could offer as an ordained minister within the Church. It was to no avail. I gradually became aware of a familiar song playing in my head with the words, 'You laid aside your majesty, gave up everything for me', and I knew that what I thought was sacrifice would actually be fulfilment and was the right next step of my becoming. However, it is somewhat sobering for me to now recall that at that time women could not actually be ordained to the priesthood.

What I do know is that since those days of intentionality about the ambition to become a speech and language therapist, there has not been another time in my life when I have had a clear map of the future. Instead, I have only recognised the seasons as they have appeared. It has not always been easy, and just as with that first call to ordination, I have often questioned whether what is being set before me is to be embraced or rejected, and I have always been grateful for the peace that has eventually come into being at each step in the journey, each of which has usually been unexpected and come at an 'inconvenient' time.

When I set aside the school nativity scene and imagine Mary in Bethlehem, I see that she had to continually lay aside her preconceived ideas about God and the Messiah as she said 'yes' to a path of faith in which every moment had to be received and lived with a heart always open to God. Mary could no longer assume what was coming next, and I believe that she clung to the God who had made promises to her ancestor, Abraham. She dared to cling to God and to wait and watch so that she was alert to recognising and receiving the signs of God's promise, which came in unexpected ways such as shepherds bursting in breathless with tales of a heavenly visitation and the promise that this baby was the Messiah. Presumably this was strangely reassuring when the promise of a royal son and an unending kingdom must have seemed rather disconnected from the experience of the moment:

> When [the shepherds] saw this, they made known what had been told them about this child; and all who heard it were amazed at what the shepherds told them. But Mary treasured all these words and pondered them in her heart. The shepherds returned, glorifying and praising God for all they had heard and seen, as it had been told them. (Luke ch.2 v.17-20)

I am certain that there were also times in Mary's life when she questioned both herself and God as she watched her son's life unfold. And when Mary eventually stood at the foot of that cross, I wonder if she was tempted to contemplate whether it had all gone horribly wrong. It must have been tortuous to watch her son experience the hatred of those around him as she watched him spat on, stabbed and nails driven through his hands and feet. What now of those distant words of Gabriel?

However, I believe that Mary never forgot the shepherds and the angels, including that extraordinary visit from Gabriel. There had also been the visit to the temple at her time of purification when she and Joseph had encountered the old man

Simeon who had been another to recognise the baby Jesus as the Messiah.[4] He had foreseen that one day Mary's heart would be pierced and I believe that as Mary stood at the foot of the cross, she would have recalled those words of Simeon. All those years ago Mary had stored the treasure in her heart and mind, and as the tears fell and she was ripped apart inside, I'm sure that she clung on to God because at the very beginning in that encounter with Gabriel, Mary's 'yes' had lit a flame that could never be put out by the darkness of despair and evil.

Mary had learnt that life is not always what it seems and there needs to be a constant letting go as we repeatedly confirm our 'yes' to God.

Every year when men and women being ordained deacon or priest are given the opportunity of saying yes to God's call on their life in a public act of worship, I am aware of my voice quivering as a I struggle to say the episcopal words which are so deeply true: 'You cannot bear the weight of this calling in your own strength, but only by the grace and power of God.'

I was grateful to hear the Archbishop of Canterbury say them to me at my consecration, yet sometimes it is only in my stumbling and falling that I let the power of them infiltrate my being. Then I am reminded to unclench my hands and let go of the plans devised in my own strength and turn my face once more to God. It is the time to try to voice another 'yes' in a place of dependence acknowledging that 'the Lord is God. It is he that has made us and we are his; we are his people and the sheep of his pasture.' (Psalm 100)

Prayer

> I am no longer my own but yours.
> Put me to what you will,
> rank me with whom you will;
> put me to doing,
> put me to suffering;
> let me be employed for you,

---

[4] Luke 2:34-35.

or laid aside for you,
exalted for you,
or brought low for you;
let me be full,
let me be empty,
let me have all things,
let me have nothing:
I freely and wholeheartedly yield all things
to your pleasure and disposal.
And now, glorious and blessed God,
Father, Son and Holy Spirit,
you are mine and I am yours. So be it.
And the covenant now made on earth, let it be
ratified in heaven.

The Methodist Covenant Prayer

NOTES

Chapter 2

THE SEEING OF
THE HEART

The next day John again was standing with two of his disciples, and as he watched Jesus walk by, he exclaimed, 'Look, here is the Lamb of God!' The two disciples heard him say this, and they followed Jesus. When Jesus turned and saw them following, he said to them, 'What are you looking for?' They said to him, 'Rabbi' (which translated means Teacher), 'where are you staying?' He said to them, 'Come and see.' (John 1:35-39)

'Seeing' and 'dwelling' are themes that ripple repeatedly through Scripture, not least in John's gospel. When Philip first comes onto the scene, he is found by Jesus, and in time Philip finds Nathanael and tells him that they have found the one of whom the prophets spoke.[5] As we hear Nathanael's scepticism and doubt about someone whose original dwelling place was Nazareth, so too we hear Philip's response, 'Come and see', which echoes these words of Jesus in these verses in John 1. Presumably there was an actual physical place where Jesus was staying but the deep invitation from Jesus to John the Baptist's disciples is to encounter him who is God come to dwell among us in flesh and blood, as declared in the opening verses of this chapter.

The recurring focus on seeing is about much more than physical sight and acknowledging what is immediately apparent in the foreground and on the surface. This is about a noticing that

[5]   John 1:43-46

involves the heart. It is about recognising God at work and it is about seeing ourselves. It is about seeing so that transformation can take place as we continue to become at home with God.

This seeing is what Jesus is constantly inviting when he tells parables — stories that shine a light in uneasy but familiar places so that we might see differently, make connections and allow restoration to take place in our inner being such that our relationship with God and neighbour can be transformed. 'See these workers' in the vineyard implies Jesus; 'see these people's reaction to an injured traveller on a road frequented by robbers'; 'see these sons and their father'; 'see these people in relation to something they've lost' — and then see yourself more clearly and discover what it means to truly dwell with God.

As I reflected on this encounter between Jesus and his first followers, and the invitation to 'come and see' and discover a place of dwelling, my mind made an unexpected connection with a church pantomime many years ago. The place was St George's Tufnell Park in Islington and the year was 1998. My years there as a curate and Associate Vicar were coming to an end and I was preparing to move to a new post and move house.

Every December during those years at St George's, the carols, candles and retelling of God coming to earth to pitch his tent among us[6] were always preceded by the excitement and exhaustion of the church pantomime.

This involved living with a lot of external mess around the church building as scenery was built and costumes were created, but that was only what could be seen on the surface. It didn't take much looking to see the more complex mess of human interaction. Rehearsals provoked both laughter and tears as amid the fun and camaraderie the intensity exposed people's pride, ambition, fear of failure and desire to be valued. There were those who yearned to be part of the action but lacked confidence or who wrongly assumed they wouldn't be wanted. There were also those who compared the length of their appearance on stage with that of others as if it implied

---

[6] John 1, *The Message.*

a pecking order of importance. Then there were those who expressed dissatisfaction with their costume, seeing it as perhaps too plain or too exotic.

For me this was the stuff of community, as people of all ages and diverse backgrounds rubbed shoulders with one another and revealed inner gold and dross whilst participating together on the stage, behind the scenes and as the audience. Local people crowded into the church building for each performance, eager to see. There was always the criticism of a few regarding the inappropriateness of using a space built for Christian worship to air the panto dame and the wince-inducing jokes, but the wonderful truth was that people were crossing the threshold of the church building to participate in an event in which life and story were celebrated, and where people were invited to 'come and see'. This was holy ground and God was present.

As people participated in the pantomime they entered into a story in which good always triumphs over evil, and in which the characters of light and goodness always triumph over the wicked and abusive. In a pantomime, love always wins the day. Furthermore, in a place of welcome and inclusion there was always an explicit invitation to return in the December days ahead to come and see yet more and to be open to the possibility of encountering God who came to earth in fragile human form to dwell among us.

The mystery and adventure of preparation and rehearsal as well as the performances acted out on a stage with painted landscape, always held the possibility of connecting with the interior landscape of people's lives, not unlike Jesus' parables, as people watched and were enabled to see more clearly.

The final panto production before I left the church to become a vicar was *The Wizard of Oz* – a pantomime about following, although it was the yellow brick road and not the dusty roads and fields of first-century Palestine.

The Wizard of Oz is one of those stories that richly fed my imagination as a child and is also one of those stories I quite frequently refer to when discussing spirituality, because it not only speaks of adventure, discovery and the mysterious unknown, but it is a story of following, of searching, of encounter and of becoming.

In that pantomime in 1998 I opted for a small walk-on part, due to the fact that I had a lot going on in anticipation of leaving. And so it was that I was cast as the Wicked Witch of the East – a pun on the fact that I was moving to the east end of London to become vicar of St James-the-Less, Bethnal Green. Incidentally, it was at the time when the controversial Millennium Dome (Now The O2) was being built to contain the Millennium Experience at the turn of the twenty-first century. My costume included a headpiece made of an upturned basin covered in silver foil with silver-sprayed sticks protruding from it thus reflecting the shape of the iconic Greenwich landmark.

In the story of *The Wizard of Oz*, distinctive characters encounter one another and choose to embark on a journey together to find the kingdom of Oz. It is a journey marked by personal fear and desire; longing and hope. And how the characters see themselves reveals their brokenness and dis-ease as much as all that is to be admired and applauded. The Scarecrow longs for a brain, the Tin Man desires a heart and the Lion wants courage, and in their searching and longing the characters discover that the answer to what they are seeking lies within them, but they had not seen it.

All of this resonates strongly with a campaign I have been involved with since 2016, which is about how young people see themselves and are susceptible to the myths of advertising and social media which predominantly focus on what can be seen on the surface rather than the heart of who people are.

In 2016, The *Good Childhood Report* produced by The Children's Society highlighted that more than a third of girls were unhappy with their appearance and that this was identifiable as an underlying cause of low self-esteem and poor mental health. Similarly the Girlguiding's *Girls' Attitudes Survey,* found that girls as young as seven were saying that they felt embarrassed and ashamed of how they looked.

I was deeply perturbed by these findings, which starkly revealed a seemingly dominant discourse around perfection that is not focussed on our internal landscapes, but is all about external, physical appearance. It is also important to add that this is not an issue exclusive to girls.

With the commitment and vision of the Diocese of Gloucester communications team, I began a campaign under the heading 'Liedentity' to add my voice to all those speaking out against the message that our worth is all about our physical appearance.

Over the past few years there have been visits to schools and colleges, a national conference and several opportunities to add my voice to national discussion and debate around issues ranging from social media to mental health.

While so much of the conversation and interaction with young people has been about focusing on their unique value, I am also clear that the mystery of becoming is not just about focusing on the individual. It is only in relationship that our brokenness and our gifts are disclosed and we discover our potential and what it means to flourish. It's even there in the story of the *Wizard of Oz*.

This truth of needing to hold the focus on the individual within the necessary surrounding water of relationship, touches on one of the ongoing debates around social media. It can undoubtedly be a gift in the developing and sustaining of relationship, but it can also detract from the depths of relationship and create a focus on the individual in which self-perception becomes distorted due to the judgement by others or of self.

At the start of the Liedentity campaign I was invited to appear on *BBC Breakfast* to talk about why as a bishop in the Church of England I was giving time to this. One of the presenters quite rightly pointed out that when my generation were teenagers we too were anxious about our bodies and being seen as physically acceptable. I agreed that issues of body image in the context of self-worth are nothing new, yet, as I continually point out, when I was a tall teenager with size eight feet and acne I did not have the pressure of social media. Neither I nor other people were posting photos of me leaving me anxious about whether they would attract 'likes' or vitriolic comments. Furthermore I had been fortunate to have family, friends and adults around me at home, church and school who affirmed me for who I was and who I was becoming.

During my 2019 sabbatical, I hosted a reunion of a small group of some of those friends from my teenage years at Broxbourne School – a local comprehensive and mixed secondary school. Our contact with each other had been sporadic over the years, but with a bit of networking some of the class of 1981 plus three teachers gathered over lunch in the garden at Bishopscourt.

Inevitably as people arrived immediate comments were about appearance and whether or not people had changed, and yet that quickly segued into a desire to hear the headlines of people's stories and get a sense of who people had become. Amid people trying on my old school blazer (which for some reason is still in my wardrobe) there was also the inevitable passing round of photographs including formal class photographs, a photograph outside Buckingham Palace following the presentation of Gold Duke of Edinburgh awards and various snaps of school trips. I was fairly horrified at my appearance in these photos, and what felt like a stark lack of physical beauty seen alongside some of the other girls. For a few brief moments, I was back in touch with those feelings of inadequacy as a teenager when I looked in the mirror. Yet the even stronger feeling in the garden that day was of gratitude for friendship, which truly was more than skin deep. That acceptance and support of one another in our different gifts and personalities that had been present over 40 years ago was tangibly present once again in our conversations over lunch, as we reminisced and laughed over memories – many of which highlighted our weaknesses, and yet reflected our acceptance of one another.

It was not difficult to remember who had been academic or who had excelled at sport or music. I was struck once again by how different we had all been and the diverse paths we had taken after school, yet there had been a sense of belonging to each other and of caring for each other – what I would now recognise as a genuine desire to enable one another to go on becoming. And it was so easily rekindled in the present as we heard fragments of each other's stories and entered into people's celebratory highlights, as well as empathising with stories of pain.

I was also struck by the fact we had gathered from across the country and that very few of us still have family in the Broxbourne area, even though at one time it had been home for all of us and had been our place of connection and setting out into life.

On that evening of the reunion, after people had left and I was clearing up, I found myself wishing that there had been more time together to go even deeper with each other and discover more of people's personal heart journeys. That night I prayed that we might each have glimpsed something new of God in our encounters with each other and that there might have been some gentle blowing on the sparks of God's love within us.

From the different gospel narratives we glean that Jesus' first followers left their physical homes, although when Jesus invited them to 'come and see' they did not expect the road to lead them to Jesus' death and even less so to a place of resurrection. It was only after Jesus' ascension and the subsequent coming of the Holy Spirit to indwell them that those first disciples could look back and begin to truly see and recognise that it was a journey of the heart and that it was about discovering the kingdom of God and seeing differently.

Prayer

O gracious and Holy Father,
give us wisdom to perceive thee,
intelligence to understand thee,
diligence to seek thee,
patience to wait for thee,
eyes to behold thee,
a heart to meditate upon thee, and
a life to proclaim thee; through
the power of the Spirit of Jesus Christ our Lord.

(Benedict 480 – 543)

NOTES

Chapter 3

THE WET
FOOTPRINTS
OF OUR BAPTISM

As Jesus passed along the Sea of Galilee, he saw Simon and his brother Andrew casting a net into the lake— for they were fishermen. And Jesus said to them, 'Follow me and I will make you fish for people.' And immediately they left their nets and followed him. As he went a little farther, he saw James son of Zebedee and his brother John, who were in their boat mending the nets. Immediately he called them; and they left their father Zebedee in the boat with the hired men, and followed him. (Mark 1:16-20)

Perhaps we have become so familiar with the gospel account of Jesus calling his first followers that we have ceased to be amazed that Jesus didn't go about his task of assembling an initial group of followers by knocking on the doors of the wealthy or by going into the synagogue in search of the religious leaders. Jesus went among the ordinary people going about their everyday business, and for Simon and Andrew, James and John the context of their everyday lives was fishing.

The scene intrigues me and whenever I hear this gospel reading I find myself wondering what conversation went on beyond the few words presented by the gospel writers. What on earth did James and John say to their father Zebedee, and what on earth did those fishermen actually envisage in terms of what they were doing?

What I do know is that as they left their boats they would undoubtedly have been fairly soggy from the water, and they would have left a few wet footprints as they began their following.

As I stepped through the great West doors of Gloucester Cathedral at the start of my service of inauguration as Bishop of Gloucester in September 2015, I was met by a young person at the font who greeted me in the name of Christ and posed questions to me about my name and purpose. My response began with the words, 'I am Rachel, a pilgrim and servant of Jesus: I have come as one seeking the grace of God so that, journeying together as the fellowship of the baptised and the body of Christ, we may proclaim the love of God and that he may be worshipped, trusted and adored by all.'

I was then sprinkled with water by a child to remind me of my baptism into Christ. Having foolishly told her at the rehearsal to splash me with confidence, she proceeded to almost drench me and I suspect there were quite a few drips as I began my journey down the aisle of the cathedral.

The symbolism was not lost on me when I came to preach my sermon, using words that I continue to repeat on many occasions and in different settings. The words are those of the twenty-first-century theologian, Michael Jinkins. Writing about Christian baptism he says: 'we are soaked to the skin in the death of Christ. Our union with Christ drips from us.... We trail wet footprints of this drenching wherever we go; we never dry off'.[7]

That image of trailing the wet footprints of our baptism is a repeated motif in my passion for encouraging followers of Christ to live out their faith in who they are among the people and places of everyday life.

I believe that one of the greatest challenges for us as Christ's Church is to understand our identity as the Church which is gathered and sent. In a simplistic way I talk about *doing* church and *being* church. *Doing* church is what we do when we gather together for worship or gatherings such as home groups. Such

---

[7] *The Church Faces Death*, p. 23.

gathered worship includes confession, spoken and sung prayer and praise, nurturing and nourishing in scripture and bread and wine. And at the end of gathered worship we are sent out in the power of God's spirit 'to live and work to God's praise and glory'.[8]

In the Anglican Church, those who have gathered for worship are frequently dismissed in the name of Christ with words such as 'go in peace to love and serve the Lord'. It is a sad indictment on us if that sending goes no further than the coffee and refreshments after the service or if it is only about activity that involves a rota.

'Being church' is about who we are as we continue to go on becoming who we have been called to be – it is about authentic daily living as a disciple in places of pain and struggle as well as places of ease and joy.

When Jesus spoke about his followers being a seasoning of salt throughout our world; the shining of light in places of immense pain and struggle; being the fragrance of Christ wherever we are and whatever we are doing, it wasn't a menu of options. It was and is a given. And it is about the whole people of God.

As a Church we have got in a muddle and mess around the language of vocation and ministry, and sadly in the Church of England those services that are about ordination, licensing or commissioning so often fail to reflect that whatever is being marked in the lives of individuals is actually about the whole people of God.

In the Church of England, this truth is captured in the opening words of the ordination service and for me it is important that this is clearly underlined in the way the service is conducted, not least ensuring a diversity of participation:

God calls his people to follow Christ, and forms us into a royal priesthood, a holy nation, to declare the wonderful deeds of him who has called us out of darkness into his marvellous light ... The Church is the Body of Christ, the

---

8   Prayer after Communion, *Common Worship*, © The Archbishops' Council.

people of God and the dwelling-place of the Holy Spirit. In baptism the whole Church is summoned to witness to God's love and to work for the coming of his kingdom.'[9]

Within the Church, there are those people who have a strong sense of living out a vocation in a particular place and at a particular time, but it is not about ordination or licensing. For example there are people who speak of living out their vocation as parents or carers, or in a profession or sport, or in using their gifts in many different contexts perhaps as enablers and healers. There are also those people who do not feel that what they do Sunday through to Saturday is fulfilling a sense of vocation, and this can be a source of pain, frustration or disappointment, yet those people of all ages and backgrounds are no lesser disciples. Just as every follower of Christ is a member of the one body with no parts being disregarded by another, so every follower of Christ is an ambassador for Christ with no one being less significant than another:

'So if anyone is in Christ, there is a new creation: everything old has passed away; see, everything has become new! ... All this is from God, who reconciled us to himself through Christ, and has given us the ministry of reconciliation...' (2 Corinthians 5:17-18)

And so, says Paul, 'We are ambassadors for Christ, since God is making his appeal through us... ' (2 Corinthians 5:20)

When I was an Archdeacon in the Diocese of London and we were discerning the next five years of our diocesan vision (Capital Vision 2020), I was a strong advocate for a focus on everyday faith, and enabling clergy to live their calling in nurturing and supporting followers of Christ to live faith among the people and places of daily life, rather than always trying to identify people who can take on tasks

---

[9]   The Greeting, Ordination Service, *Common Worship*, © The Archbishops' Council.

and ministries within the activity of 'doing church'.

Thus it was that I became a sponsor for a strand of the diocesan vision called 'ambassadors for Christ' which was about shining a spotlight on celebrating and commissioning people to understand themselves as Christ's ambassadors among the people and places of their everyday lives.[10] I confess that I was less keen on the decision to count and record all those who were commissioned, as I thought such measuring was a distraction from the need to focus on culture change and impact. I am far more excited by the life in the leaven which impacts the appearance, size and taste of the dough, than I am in measuring the leaven, which might be ineffective. To continue the theme of that kingdom of God image from Jesus,[11] 'the proof of the pudding is in the eating'.

This commitment to nurturing everyday faith is reflected in our diocesan vision in Gloucester and in my involvement with national endeavours to enable and support culture change across the Church of England.

A question I go on asking myself as a Bishop is, how do I enable people to see their whole lives through a 'kingdom of God-shaped' lens, and how can I actively challenge any collusion with a false understanding of discipleship which suggests that it is primarily about activity focused on the gathered worshipping community?

I suspect that many of us are familiar with stories of people who recount how they had been prayed for in church because they were part of 'doing church' activity (such as the church council or the children's activities or part of the welcome team), but had never been prayed for in their everyday role as a teacher or a cleaner or a grandparent or whatever it might be.

I am not proposing that corporate prayer and worship is insignificant in who we are as the Church as we seek to give God glory and grow in faith and love. Indeed, the Church is a Eucharistic community, the body of Christ, which gathers amid

---

[10] 2 Corinthians 5:20.
[11] Matthew 13:33 and Luke 13:20-21.

the brokenness of the world and the brokenness of our lives, to break bread and be fed by Christ. And from that place of gathering we are sent out to be Christ's body and nourish the world. What I am proposing is that we go on pushing at the boundaries of how people understand themselves as individuals and as the body of Christ in this life of being gathered and sent. It is about constantly trying to keep the kingdom of God as the big picture.

One of the things I said at my inauguration as Bishop of Gloucester was that I would endeavour to invite people to introduce themselves to me not in relation to their 'doing church' activity but rather in relation to the people and places of their daily lives. For example, rather than someone introducing themselves as a churchwarden they might introduce themselves to me as a volunteer in the local charity shop or perhaps as an orthopaedic surgeon or a careworker or a grandparent who helps their son with the grandchildren; or possibly as someone currently undergoing chemotherapy and spending a lot of time in a hospital waiting room. It has not been easy and I have often had to push quite hard to get beyond people listing the things that they do connected with 'doing church'. In all of this I am still very much wanting to fan the flames of how worshipping communities are engaged with the wider community, but I also want each of us to broaden our horizons when it comes to the landscape of where and how we are being *ambassadors for Christ*.

Certainly, in the Church of England it is all there in the words and theology of our liturgy, but we are not always good at acknowledging it when people come together for public worship, gathered in from the people and places of daily life carrying an array of joys and struggles. At the end of our gathered worship how do we acknowledge that when we are sent out 'to live and work to God's praise and glory' it is about being who we are amid our lives in different places and among different people and with a whole spectrum of thoughts and feelings?

How do our public intercessions or our conversations over after-service refreshments acknowledge people's daily lives and express interest and care about what people are facing, doing and being? In all the places where we each live out our lives Sunday through to Saturday, are our hearts expectant for those around us to encounter Christ in us and through us by the mysterious work of the Holy Spirit? Indeed, do we ourselves expect to encounter God in unexpected ways in the places of our daily lives, including the uncomfortable places?

In chapter 5, I write of a beach in North Wales and the nurturing of my faith in childhood. It was far from the shores of Galilee, yet in the vicinity of the small town of Criccieth some serious fishing did take place, but most of it was about crabbing in rock pools with little nets bought from the corner shop. Yet just as with the shore of Galilee for the first followers of Jesus Christ, that beach was a formative place for me. Here at a young age I encountered Jesus and discovered that my relationship with God was not restricted to church buildings, but rather was about the places of my everyday life.

I discovered that too in another formative place led by an individual who lived out God's love in daily life. The place was a nursery just outside Stockport and the person was Grace Wyatt. More than 50 years ago Grace was a young mother who was challenged about how she could live out her Christian faith in deeper ways within her community. As a mother of young children, she decided to open her home as a playgroup to local parents and their children. This included those labelled 'disabled' who were usually excluded from places of play and learning established only with their 'able' peers in mind.

The playgroup grew quickly and moved into new accommodation, and in 1973 the Charnwood Trust came into being.

As a sixth-former, I had the privilege of being part of a summer residential organised by Scripture Union, which gathered young people together to assist with the running of a holiday family play scheme at the nursery. We planned activities for the children and joined in with the practicalities of their everyday routines. I loved the interaction with children and adults alike and it confirmed my desire to become a paediatric speech and language therapist.

It is only now as I look back that I realise how influential Grace was in my life. She was a woman who was passionate about every person being precious, loved by God and of equal worth, and was someone who created spaces for relationship and discovery, all rooted in her own encounter with Christ and her call to follow which was about everyday life.

In Grace I encountered someone who most definitely left wet footprints of her baptism wherever she went, and in recent months I have wondered how much of who I am has been shaped by Grace Wyatt and am sad that I never took the opportunity to tell her that whilst she was still alive on earth.

Prayer

Christ has no body now but yours. No hands, no feet on earth but yours. Yours are the eyes through which he looks compassion on this world. Yours are the feet with which he walks to do well. Yours are the hands through which he blesses all the world. Yours are the hands, yours are the feet, yours are the eyes, and you are his body. Christ has no body now on earth but yours.

Teresa of Avila

NOTES

Chapter 4

TASTING THE KINGDOM OF GOD

On the third day there was a wedding in Cana of Galilee, and the mother of Jesus was there. Jesus and his disciples had also been invited to the wedding. When the wine gave out, the mother of Jesus said to him, 'They have no wine.' And Jesus said to her, 'Woman, what concern is that to you and to me? My hour has not yet come.' His mother said to the servants, 'Do whatever he tells you.' Now standing there were six stone water-jars for the Jewish rites of purification, each holding twenty or thirty gallons. Jesus said to them, 'Fill the jars with water.' And they filled them up to the brim. He said to them, 'Now draw some out, and take it to the chief steward.' So they took it. When the steward tasted the water that had become wine, and did not know where it came from (though the servants who had drawn the water knew), the steward called the bridegroom and said to him, 'Everyone serves the good wine first, and then the inferior wine after the guests have become drunk. But you have kept the good wine until now.' Jesus did this, the first of his signs, in Cana of Galilee, and revealed his glory; and his disciples believed in him (John 2:1-11)

During my time in Galilee in the summer of 2019 I went to Kufr Kana (Cana), the town named by John in the second chapter of his gospel. Here I too witnessed transformation. Not water into wine but transformed relationship and perspective as Arab and

Jewish women work together and embody a vision of peaceful coexistence in a wonderful not-for-profit organisation called Sindyanna (the local oak tree which is the most common tree in Galilee).

The women work together to produce olive oil and other food products such as Za'atar (a Middle Eastern mixture of herbs and spices). Some of them also weave baskets, and the latest project is focused on hydroponics – using water not to create exquisite wine, but to grow vegetables and herbs in tiny spaces.

Sindyanna is creating opportunities for women, supporting local growers and producers and advancing Fair Trade. Yet Sindyanna is not only transforming lives in terms of economics, it is also bringing about social transformation as Arabs and Jews build interpersonal relationships, support each other and enter into each other's stories.

For me, this reflects Kingdom of God transformation and what I encountered at Sindyanna resonates with other projects I have seen recently in both Egypt and in Bosnia (as mentioned in chapter 13).

In January 2019 I had the joy of visiting Egypt for the first time as part of an all-women group of Christians hosted by the charity 'Embrace the Middle East'. We were visiting projects with a particular focus on women and children, supported by Embrace in partnership with Egyptian Christians. All of the projects we saw were about enabling people to taste a new reality and to imagine a different future made possible through a belief in the potential of individuals and communities.

Amid a gathering of women in a community centre in one of the Zabaleen communities where people live amid huge piles of rubbish they collect and sort, we listened to women tell stories of empowerment through literacy, health and community education. These women are being confident ambassadors back in their local communities as they share their learning and are catalysts for transformation, not least where Female Genital Mutilation (FGM) is common practice.

Later, in the Egyptian desert we experienced the beauty and

tranquillity of Anaphora – a place of retreat and restoration run by a Coptic Christian community, with worship at its heart. The beautiful buildings are set among verdant vegetation watered by a carefully designed irrigation system in which the central channels are formed into the shape of a large question mark with a tiny chapel at the dot. Anaphora is not only a place to bring questions before God but also a place which enables new possibility and opens up new vistas in response to the questions of what and why and how. Here the Soteria project provides residential courses for rural Egyptian women who have experienced sexual, physical or emotional abuse. Sara, who manages the programme, says that the process of transformation 'happens woman by woman, story by story' and each woman is supported as she returns to her community to be an agent of change.

This not only reminds me of the Samaritan woman at the well (chapter 7 of this book) but it also reverberates with the transformation of that first miracle of Jesus Christ in Cana of Galilee.

At the centre of this miracle is the presence of Jesus Christ, and the scene around him contains a number of people, most of whom taste transformation, but not all recognise Jesus as the source. There were those who tasted the wine and probably, after a conversation with the servants recognised that it was Jesus who was the key to the amazing change, whilst other guests probably remained oblivious to all that had gone on but very much enjoyed drinking the wine. Perhaps in time some of them came to understand what they had tasted and even became followers of Christ, whilst others never gave the goodness on their palate another thought. There would probably have been some who never actually got to taste it. I am struck by the fact that the servants, who are the people with the lowest status in this event, presumably never got to taste the wine although they were the ones fully in the know regarding its source. Hopefully some of them went on to taste Christ's life-giving water, far richer than the best wine.

This miracle at Cana resonates so strongly with my vision for the Church's call to build community, not only within the Body of Christ but beyond, in and with the wider context in which we find ourselves.

I am passionate about participating in God's work of transformation – being those servants – knowing that giving people the opportunity to taste the wine of the kingdom is good in itself regardless of whether or not people immediately recognise Christ's touch.

This vision was key in my own calling to ordination and it is what I have endeavoured to live in ministry. So much of my parish ministry in London was about creating spaces where people could experience community, share stories and participate together in creating and tasting something life-giving that responds to people's hopes and needs.

For me, the church building hosting toddler groups, lunch and tea gatherings for older people, or English-speaking space for local Bangladeshi women, was all about the opportunity for people to taste the Kingdom of God as they discovered the gift of welcome, rest, acceptance and support.

One of my favourite initiatives was SPACE (Special Parents And Children Event). As a curate I noticed that whilst the modern church of St George's in Tufnell Park was a vast space, many local families were living in small flats. Even where there was the inclination to undertake messy craft activities the space would rarely allow it. Furthermore, I noticed that many parents and children rarely, if ever, engaged together in creative activity.

So I took the risk of advertising a very simple afterschool event which was for children accompanied by a parent or carer. Posters went up and leaflets were distributed in the local primary schools. With a small grant from a charity, large tarpaulins were purchased plus glue and paint and paper. Members of the church community donated things such as empty cereal packets, yoghurt pots and the inner tubes from toilet rolls, and several retired people signed up to help with refreshments.

The week we opened I wondered if anyone would turn up, but I was not to be disappointed. Week after week adults and children came to the church building. It was a place of physical mess as well as being a place where the mess of life was spoken about and shared over tea and toast. Amid the tears and laughter and strange-looking gluey creations, relationships were built and families and volunteers alike tasted something good in a place of community.

Furthermore, some of those families ventured into places of new inner discovery as they chose to participate in Sunday worship or Christmas services, often for the first time. There were christenings, prayers and encounter with God.

When I moved on to St James the Less, Bethnal Green, I was glad that SPACE was replicated, although in a slightly different way.

I always hope that amid relationship and interaction, just as at that wedding in Cana, people will discover something good and unexpected. That in a place of community people might come to see Jesus Christ as the source of that goodness and desire to taste something more. Yet, it is important that the wine is tasted and offered freely regardless of understanding and recognition of God.

It is also important that such hospitality and gift is not about self-righteous Christians doing things 'for' other people, who are somehow perceived as the ones in need, but that it is about creating something good *with* other people and sometimes with other organisations, which is about everyone giving and everyone receiving as community is formed and transformed. All of us are people in need and each of us has something to give. We are all invited to drink and taste.

In that wedding party narrative everyone seems to be involved and playing their part, even the guests in their enjoyment of the wine. No doubt their compliments to the bridegroom, servants and steward provided affirmation and satisfaction.

When I encounter community ministry of 'with', it makes my soul sing.

I remember the first time I visited a winter night shelter when I was Archdeacon of Northolt. A number of worshipping communities in Brent in North West London had formed a local initiative to provide seven-nights-a-week shelter and food throughout the winter for those who were experiencing homelessness. Over the years the initiative expanded across many London boroughs and each night homeless guests were hosted in a different church building and provided with an evening meal, a warm place to sleep with bedding provided, and breakfast in the morning.

On this particular occasion I went along to join the guests and volunteers for an evening meal, and as I walked into the hubbub of conversation as people sat together around a large table I realised that I couldn't immediately identify who were the guests and who were the official volunteers. In reality people were participating in different ways as they contributed to the organisation and gathering, and everyone seemed to be receiving. Here was a glimpse of God's invitation to a spacious table and a foretaste of the heavenly banquet.

At the inception of the project it had not been easy to recruit enough volunteers due to people's anxieties and misperceptions, yet once people had seen what had unfolded there were almost too many volunteers because people wanted to taste something of the ordinary becoming the extraordinary.

In my time as an archdeacon and now as a bishop I have experienced so many examples of worshipping communities seeking to identify the hopes and needs in their wider communities and then creating something, often in partnership with other individuals and organisations, which tastes good and is transforming for all those who participate. I'm delighted that in the Diocese of Gloucester we are continuing to discover how art, music and sport can build relationship and be infused with the love and hope of Jesus Christ. It is my hope that the dream of creating new worshipping communities in and through physical activity including local community sports centres, will become a reality and enable children and adults who have not yet tasted the wine of the kingdom of God to do so.

Likewise, it is my hope and prayer that the women released from prison who are able to be reunited with their children in one of our diocesan houses might taste something extraordinary and encounter transformation.[12] I also pray that they will be drawn to recognise the transforming touch of Christ.

One of the projects that stands out for me from my time as Archdeacon of Hackney in East London was that of the Cantignorous chorus. Initiated by a local vicar and a Christian musician, it brought together a number of diverse people, many of whom were participants in groups that used the church hall during the week. This included people currently homeless, a charity working with vulnerable women, an over-fifties dance group and Narcotics Anonymous. In their first season of meeting in 2014, the choir recorded a single that included choristers from St Paul's Cathedral. I had the privilege of being at the recording – it was chaotic, raw and inspiring. I glimpsed the Kingdom hallmarks of unity and community, and as we shared in refreshments together before and after the recording, I tasted something far richer and more exquisite than the flavour of the physical food and drink.

A common thread in so many of the examples I have given is about transformation in and with people who often feel they are pushed to the edges of life, or are perceived that way by those who seemingly occupy the central spaces of life. The transforming touch of Christ removes separation and builds community which signposts the Kingdom of God, and it connects with those water jars in Cana.

We know that those jars were for water to be used for purification. Ritual cleansing was a necessary part of Jewish life, not least when someone had seemingly been tainted through such acts as touching a menstruating woman or being touched by a leper or relating to prostitutes and tax collectors. Yet all these seemingly 'unclean' acts were things Jesus did to demonstrate love and inclusion in the kingdom of God. This is the rich wine which Jesus wanted people to taste and although that first miracle revealing God's glory took place at a celebratory event, it is often in a place of pain and desolation that we can find ourselves tasting the wine of the kingdom of God.

[12]   In conjunction with The Nelson Trust Re-unite Gloucestershire project.

Prayer

Almighty God,
in Christ you make all things new;
transform the poverty of our nature
by the riches of your grace,
and in the renewal of our lives
make known your heavenly glory;
through Jesus Christ your Son our Lord
who is alive and reigns with you in the unity of the Holy
    Spirit,
one God now and for ever. **Amen**

(Collect for the Second Sunday of Epiphany)[13]

[13] *Common Worship*, © The Archbishops' Council.

NOTES

Chapter 5

PLACE AND NAME

> They came to the other side of the sea, to the country
> of the Gerasenes. And when he had stepped out of the
> boat, immediately a man out of the tombs with an
> unclean spirit met him. He lived among the tombs;
> and no one could restrain him any more, even with a
> chain; for he had often been restrained with shackles
> and chains, but the chains he wrenched apart, and the
> shackles he broke in pieces; and no one had the strength
> to subdue him. Night and day among the tombs and
> on the mountains he was always howling and bruising
> himself with stones. When he saw Jesus from a distance,
> he ran and bowed down before him; and he shouted at
> the top of his voice, 'What have you to do with me, Jesus,
> Son of the Most High God? I adjure you by God, do not
> torment me.' For he had said to him, 'Come out of the
> man, you unclean spirit!' Then Jesus asked him, 'What is
> your name?' He replied, 'My name is Legion; for we are
> many.' He begged him earnestly not to send them out
> of the country. Now there on the hillside a great herd of
> swine was feeding; and the unclean spirits begged him,
> 'Send us into the swine; let us enter them.' So he gave
> them permission. And the unclean spirits came out and
> entered the swine; and the herd, numbering about two
> thousand, rushed down the steep bank into the sea, and
> were drowned in the sea. (Mark 5:1-13)

This strange and uncomfortable encounter in the Gospel of
Mark confronts me with the God who is beyond understanding
and yet deeply personal. Here is our mysterious God who is

more powerful than the principalities and powers of evil and yet who knows me by name and invites me to participate in the adventure of the Kingdom of God.

Yet in all the intimacy, this story is neither cosy nor neat. It disturbs me and leaves me with questions I cannot answer, not least around demon possession. It takes me to the dark places of life and yet it energises me as I see the potential for transformation even amid mess, questions and turbulence. Here is the big picture that God is making all things new and at the heart of what God is about is restoration and relationship.

As with all encounters this event took place in a specific place, and during my sabbatical time in Galilee we visited the beach at Kursi close to the place presented as the site of these events as told by Mark.

As I look back on my life, I am aware of many places I would name as significant with one of the earliest being another beach, not in Galilee but in North Wales.

During my pre-school and primary school years my family spent two weeks every August in Criccieth. It was always planned to coincide with the period of the beach mission, originally run by CSSM (Children's Special Service Mission) and then by Scripture Union.

Every year we stayed in the same flat above the home of a family of a fisherman. I remember once going out mackerel fishing with him and being horribly seasick.

On those beach mission holidays, I eagerly arose from bed each morning to go along to one of the local chapels where we were gathered in age groups to read the Bible using little booklets of notes produced by Scripture Union. The Bible came alive and seemed relevant to my everyday experiences.

I don't remember the words 'should' and 'ought' but I do recall children and adults who wanted to spend time with me and talk about Jesus Christ. Each morning there was a beach gathering for people of all ages. We met in front of a sand edifice decorated with shells and flowers and our time together included a story from the Bible, prayers, songs and quizzes. Here in a very public place amid stripy beach towels, picnics, windbreakers and sandcastles, people were talking about Jesus and all whilst we were enjoying ourselves on holiday.

What I discovered was that as well as talking *about* Jesus I could talk *to* Jesus and in terms of place, nowhere is out of bounds for Jesus Christ and the work of the Holy Spirit. Indeed, in this encounter in Luke's narrative Jesus is in an uncomfortable place for a Jew. He is in 'foreign' Gentile territory and among keepers of pigs. Yet the physical landscape is only part of the story. It is the internal landscape where the deep change took place for the man.

As I look back on my life I can recall significant encounters with God, whether alone or with other people, which have taken place in specific locations and often in uncomfortable places, but the interior landscape of my heart and mind is where the death and transformation continues to be realised. For example, during my time in parish ministry I remember an encounter in a hospital which was an uncomfortable place to be but where the touch of God within me was powerful and charged with life.

It had begun with a phone call and the wavering voice of a mother I knew, telling me that the baby growing in her womb had Downs Syndrome and that she and her husband had decided to terminate the pregnancy. The mother was to be induced the next day. She was clear on the phone that this was not about asking my opinion or seeking my reassurance; it was a request to be present at the birth and to pray for the child.

It was one of those occasions in which my heart responded before my head and I promised to be there. And then came the head and an influx of moral and ethical questions and thoughts. What on earth did I think I was doing? By saying yes was I implicitly providing a comforting presence which could be interpreted as endorsing a decision with which I emphatically disagreed?

Being in that hospital was almost an intolerable place to be and yet it was the space within me where the real turbulence, questioning and discovery was located. When the tiny baby appeared I knew why I was there. I was there to bear witness to this unique life, passing from life to death to life. I watched the little embryonic being kick its last in the amniotic sac, and then I held the still small human form in an oversized white blanket. Outwardly my cheeks were wet with tears whilst inwardly I was flooded with intense and conflicting emotions. In it all I knew that this tiny human being was embraced by God, and I was overwhelmed by an intermingling of death and resurrection in my belief that God's heart of love was surging with both pain and hope.

The tiny child was never named by the parents but what came into my mind were those Old Testament words in the Book of Isaiah about God being like a mother.[14] Even if a mother can forget her child it is not so with God, and I knew that there was a holy name for that little person written on the palms of God's hands.

In this uncomfortable encounter between Jesus and the man in a state of turbulence and distress, we hear Jesus asking the man 'what is your name?'.

The local community have viewed this man as a marginalised 'other' but Jesus sees him as a distinctive individual with a past and a future, created in the image of God.

Interestingly, although we hear the man describe his name as Legion (the implication being that there were many demons) we don't actually discover his real name – but we do know that he was a unique individual living in a particular place and context (and perhaps the reference to legion was a dig at Roman occupation).

One of the aspects of my episcopal ministry which I find both moving and humbling is that of confirming people of different ages and from diverse backgrounds as they make a public stand about their decision to follow Christ.

At the point of confirmation I ask each person to speak the name by which they are known, and as I mark them with the sign of the cross on their forehead and look them in the eyes, I speak their name followed by the words, 'God has called you by

---

[14]   Isaiah 49:15-16.

name and made you his own'. In those few moments of word and sign there is a wordless acknowledgement that before me stands a precious individual, created by God who knows their story and context, and sees glory, fracture and potential as they go on becoming.

In our calling to live as people of relationship our name is very important. As I think back to that beach mission in Criccieth I remember at about the age of three or four, making a huge name badge and decorating it. I began to learn that as with every person ever conceived I am unique, that God knows me as I am, loves me and wants me to go on becoming the person I have been created to be.

This realisation about each person's precious worth and equal value provides an energy that motivates me in my ministry not least in my engagement with those who often don't feel valued or whose self-esteem is low or who perceive themselves to be a shunned 'other'. This is the fire that has burned within me in recent months and years when encountering people such as women in prison, or with families with disabled children, or with the Zabaleen communities working on the rubbish heaps in Egypt, or with a group of men without homes and living on the streets in Gloucester, or with a group of local young people who see their worth as rooted in their appearance. Each of them has a name and as with every human being, past, present and future they are each fearfully and wonderfully made[15] and imprinted with the divine spark.

Just as I find it poignant to mark confirmation candidates with an oily cross, so too I find it poignant on Ash Wednesday to have my own forehead marked with a cross of ash and to mark others similarly, speaking the words, 'Remember that you are dust, and to dust you shall return.' We are all equal as human beings and regardless of our status or privilege, one day every person's mortal flesh will return to dust.

In March 2019 I made a brief visit to Bosnia as part of a small group of Christian women hosted by the organisation

[15] Psalm 139.

'Remembering Srebrenica'. It was deeply moving on Ash Wednesday to visit the Srebrenica–Potočari Memorial and Cemetery where many of the bodies are buried, following the abhorrent act of genocide in Srebrenica in July 1995 in which about eight thousand Muslim men and boys were brutally murdered. Earlier that day we had visited the mortuary where identifying body parts through painstaking DNA analysis continues as body parts are found. This horrific dismembering of bodies arose as a result of the original mass graves being dug up by machinery in order to destroy the evidence and transfer body parts to scattered places of burial.

Being in the mortuary surrounded by body bags was a heavy reminder of our mortality and the dust of human flesh. It was therefore amid tears that I stood in the fading light and marked each of our group with an ash cross. We prayed and sang in an attitude of repentance and lament.

In the episode in Mark's gospel in the country of the Gerasenes, the man who has been a distanced 'other' encounters Jesus in a particular geographical location but the real locus of transformation takes place within him. Amid my own reflections I am challenged to be more deeply aware of those external places where I fail to notice that I am 'othering' people or wielding inappropriate power or colluding with people who are inappropriately deferential. Yet I know this awareness needs to begin in the interior landscape of my heart and mind so that I can go on being transformed. I also know that so much of this interior work takes place when I am in the presence of people who often feel 'other'.

I think of a recent occasion with some amazing parents and their equally inspiring children who have special needs; and of some time with a group of young people who are the primary carers of a family member whilst also upholding their studies in school and college. On both occasions I came away feeling more than a little perturbed that I was the one being seen as the 'important' guest when in reality I had been in the presence of precious individuals exhibiting resilience and courage way beyond that which I have ever shown. In my conversation with those named individuals in those different places I endeavoured to convey how they had enlivened me and would continue to do so.

Prayer

Give me a candle of the spirit, O God
as I go down into the deep of my
own being
Show me the hidden things. Take me
down to the spring of my life, and
tell me my nature and my name.
Give me freedom to grow so that I
may become my true self – the
fulfilment of the seed which you
planted in me at my making.
Out of the deep I cry unto thee, O God.
Amen

A Gathering Prayer by Bishop George Appleton
(©1974 – modern adaptation by Jim Cotter)

NOTES

Chapter 6

SHARING THE STORY

The swineherds ran off and told it in the city and in the country. Then people came to see what it was that had happened. They came to Jesus and saw the demoniac sitting there, clothed and in his right mind, the very man who had had the legion; and they were afraid. Those who had seen what had happened to the demoniac and to the swine reported it. Then they began to beg Jesus to leave their neighbourhood. As he was getting into the boat, the man who had been possessed by demons begged him that he might be with him. But Jesus refused, and said to him, 'Go home to your friends, and tell them how much the Lord has done for you, and what mercy he has shown you.' And he went away and began to proclaim in the Decapolis how much Jesus had done for him; and everyone was amazed. (Mark 5:14-20)

In this encounter it is surely understandable that the man would want to stay with Jesus; after all he has just experienced the love and power of this amazing person. So when Jesus gets back into the boat the man begs to go with him. Presumably, the man not only wants to know and experience more regarding the person of Jesus, but in Jesus he has found a potential friend who has treated him very differently from his own community. He has a sense that Jesus will keep him safe.

As I live this story in my imagination I am disquieted by an awareness that I need to stay alert to my desire for that intimacy with Christ, which can sometimes be in danger of becoming dulled by the plans, structures and processes of episcopal leadership. Too often I find myself in meetings and synods where people are talking *about* Jesus as they articulate views or propose policies whilst there is a lack of that pulsing sense of living *with* Jesus and walking in the way which unsettles and disturbs.

When Jesus tells the man from whom the demons had gone to 'go home to your friends', this is not rejection, although it might well have filled the man with fear. He must have wondered how the local people would treat him given his past history. Yet Jesus was asking him to go and live the good news of encounter with Christ as he built and rebuilt relationships in his local community and told people how much God had done for him. Once again we are back to that soil of relationship with God, neighbour and creation.

Last year I was reflecting with some curates on how they had shared their personal stories during a mission weekend in the Cotswolds that had been focused around community events which connected naturally with people's lives and contexts, e.g. a farmers' breakfast, a jazz evening and a family craft morning.

When I had first met each of the curates in their journey to ordination, I had been struck by the power and poignancy of their personal stories and yet now I was noticing how at times those stories appeared over-thought and over-filtered as they shared them with other people. The person of Christ, so present in their lives, had sometimes seemed absent or sanitised and I wondered how being ordained had influenced this.

We reflected together on how natural it is to share our thoughts and feelings about a book or film that held our attention, or an encounter with a captivating place or person, and how we rarely have an ulterior motive in that conversation other than relating the stuff of our lives with and alongside each other. Why is it then that we live conversations differently when it comes to being explicit about our relationship with Jesus Christ? And why isn't the name of Jesus Christ on my lips rather more as I share stories of daily life and ponder life's mysteries?

In that conversation we talked both about respect and offence, and were curious about our application of different filters when it came to the mentioning of faith, rather than say sport or politics.

I wondered whether there is actually an implicit selfishness rather than selflessness in our hesitancy to share our questions or speak of our experiences of Christ's love, hope and mystery in our places of both pain and joy.

I find it grating when people frame a particular conversation as 'evangelistic' such that they search for special language and formulae which so often results in a forced offering which in reality seems disrespectful to the hearer because people are no longer being fully and equally present to one another in a place of relationship.

Of course, some of this touches on our futile perception of control. We cannot control the outcomes of living in relationship as we stay present to Christ and those around us. That is the work of the Holy Spirit.

In the encounter described in Mark's gospel, after the people had seen what had happened to the man and the pigs, they ask Jesus to leave. The people present had encountered a power that was even greater than that of demonic spirits and there is something here about their fear in recognising their lack of control. Whilst they had found it difficult to contain the man in his previous condition, the community had exercised some level of control as they kept guard over the man on the margins – an 'other' bound with chains and leg irons. But now, in this event of the man's healing, the local community encounter Jesus Christ, whom they cannot control. God's work and power is disturbing their way of life.

Perhaps we need greater honesty in recognising that our reticence to share the love and hope of Christ in both spoken and unspoken ways is not always about a kindness to the people we don't wish to offend, but in truth it is sometimes more about our own fear of rejection.

In 2016 we lived a discernment process across the Diocese of Gloucester as we sought to identify the shape of our vision and the priorities God was calling us to live together. The process began with a focus on prayer and led into a number of weeks of conversation framed around some key questions. While the majority of those conversations took place within worshipping communities, including our Church of England schools, there was also strong encouragement for people to have conversations in their wider communities such as in pubs and cafes, community groups, schools and homes, and with people who would not ordinarily identify themselves as members of a Christian worshipping community.

The aim was to ascertain something of people's perspective on the Church and what they might like to see in terms of the Church being involved in local transformation. As part of this process I hosted a number of conversations at Bishopscourt, with small groups of people from the public and voluntary sector as well as local businesses.

One of my perturbing observations was that our expression of being Church within many communities is commonly seen as somewhere on a spectrum between 'nice' and 'irrelevant', but a commitment to transformation too rarely seems to create energy, excitement or opposition unless it's about reordering the interior of the church building!

I want worshipping communities to be people of welcome, hospitality and holy balm, but I also hope that engagement with injustice, hope and need will involve 'holy agitation' as we participate in God's work of transformation. As Jesus lived his ministry on earth he was far from the 'gentle Jesus, meek and mild' (as described in a hymn by Charles Wesley). Instead we see Jesus' words and actions provoking strong reaction ranging from wonder to outrage.

Interestingly, the heightened sense of urgency around the climate crisis and the increased call for action has involved much public agitating focused on a cry for transformation. It has been fanned into flame not least through the action of young people, who in 2019 inspired people of all ages and backgrounds to protest. The occupation of roads and public places became a serious inconvenience and many people begged those gathered to leave. The various uncomfortable protests around the environment have challenged me to ask how well I and all of Christ's Church are 'speaking' of God's hope and life not only in the way we cherish the earth and its resources, but also in the way we engage in conversation around climate change and take opportunities to share our experiences of all that God has done for us.

During my years as an archdeacon, I sometimes found myself

visiting parochial church councils (PCCs) to discuss issues around the upkeep of buildings or dwindling congregations. One of my key questions to people was what difference it would make to the wider community if the worshipping community didn't exist. Occasionally I was met with blank faces and bemusement around the relevance of the question leaving me feeling somewhat bleak. Another equally concerning response was a confident and contented reply of 'none'.

When I hear Jesus tell the man to tell everyone how much God has done for him I am reminded once more that, while faith and encounter with God is up-close and personal, it is not private and individualistic. Our faith is lived out in community and relationship and I am increasingly challenged about how I live with authenticity and recognise the filters I apply to my words and behaviour, filters which sometimes remove the grit that might have been the making of a pearl in my own life or the lives of those around me.

As the man returned to the city and told his story as he proclaimed what Jesus had done for him I wonder what response he got and I wonder how long the story-telling went on for and how much he strived and if he ever reached a point of wondering what on earth he was doing.

I remember the night before my ordination as a deacon in 1994. My original call to explore ordination had seemed so strong and Christ's summons had seemed so vivid. Yet as our pre-ordination retreat came to an end, I remember musing momentarily on the fact that if one day I discovered that God had been nothing but an illusion, I would have given my life to fantasy. I remember recalling those words of the Apostle Paul writing to the Christians in Corinth when he points out that if Christ has not been raised from the dead then his preaching is worthless as is the faith of the Corinthians.[16] Yet, like Paul I also knew that my faith was not futile and that I wanted to play my part in sharing the good news of Christ.

I don't recall much of the detail of the input on that diaconate ordination retreat, but I do remember the warmth and love of the retreat leader, the Revd Prebendary Alan Tanner, and

[16] 1 Corinthians 15:14-15.

I do remember meditating on the banner that hung on the wall behind him as he addressed us. The banner displayed the words from Micah 6:8: 'He has told you, O mortal, what is good; And what does the LORD require of you but to do justice, and to love kindness, and to walk humbly with your God?'

Over the years I have returned to those words again and again, and I like to imagine that they might have been known to that man who was healed in Mark's gospel narrative. I hope they might have encouraged him whenever he wondered what he should be doing in his desire to proclaim Christ and give God thanks for the work of transformation in his life.

I find myself wondering to where exactly in the local community the man in Mark's account returned, after being asked by Jesus to return home. We know from Mark that the man had not lived in a house for a long time but had been living among the tombs.

Since my ordination as a deacon I have moved house five times, but in making home in different properties and different places I have discovered that truly being at home is not about physical buildings but about being at home with God in the depths of my being. It is about God's indwelling and me paying attention to the inner rooms of my being as much as I give heed to the mess or beauty of the rooms in my physical house.

One of my favourite psalms is Psalm 121 with that promise of the Lord watching over my 'coming in and going out'. My husband Guy and I chose it to be sung by a friend during the signing of the registers at our wedding, and when I was an archdeacon I always loved speaking those words to clergy when I installed them at their service of licensing. I like to think that the man who had been possessed by demons came to know that ancient 'song of ascents' and held on to that promise as he lifted his eyes to the hills around Galilee and grew in the experience of being free and at home with God.

I also trust that the man kept his heart fleshy as he lived the vulnerability of returning to his community. At different pivotal points in my life, often when beginning a new chapter of ministry, I have sensed the need to toughen up. I remember thinking those exact words when as a single person I was about to leave my one-bedroomed curate's flat and move to a large Victorian vicarage and take on the responsibility of becoming a vicar. For so many reasons I felt that I needed to grow a bit tougher. I felt this again when I was about to become an Archdeacon. There were inevitably going to be robust conversations with people and I was about to become the first female member of the London Diocese senior staff team, which then comprised sixteen men.

On both those occasions God spoke clearly to me about keeping my heart vulnerable and fleshy: 'A new heart I will give you, and a new spirit I will put within you; and I will remove from your body the heart of stone and give you a heart of flesh.'[17] Whilst hearts of flesh feel pain, fear, sorrow, anger and loss, they also feel joy, peace, love and hope. If I am to live relationship and encounter then my heart must stay fleshy and vulnerable. It's what I see in Jesus as he encountered followers, seekers, opponents, critics and inquisitors.

I hope that the man in this episode from Mark went on to discover being at home with God within himself as he endeavoured to be faithful to Christ, and I hope his heart stayed fleshy as he encountered his community in a new way.

Prayer

Will you come and follow me if I but call your name?

Will you go where you don't know and never be the same?

Will you let my love be shown? Will you let my name be known,

will you let my life be grown in you and you in me?

Will you leave yourself behind if I but call your name?

Will you care for cruel and kind and never be the same?

Will you risk the hostile stare should your life attract or scare?

Will you let me answer prayer in you and you in me?

Will you let the blinded see if I but call your name?

---

[17] Ezekiel 36:26.

Will you set the prisoners free and never be the same?
Will you kiss the leper clean and do such as this unseen,
and admit to what I mean in you and you in me?

Will you love the 'you' you hide if I but call your name?
Will you quell the fear inside and never be the same?
Will you use the faith you've found to reshape the world
    around,
through my sight and touch and sound in you and you
    in me?

Lord your summons echoes true when you but call my
    name.
Let me turn and follow you and never be the same.
In Your company I'll go where Your love and footsteps
    show.
Thus I'll move and live and grow in you and you in me.

The Summons by John L. Bell and Graham Maule

NOTES

Chapter 7

BELOVED
DAUGHTERS

Then one of the leaders of the synagogue named Jairus
came and, when he saw him, fell at his feet and begged
him repeatedly, 'My little daughter is at the point of
death. Come and lay your hands on her, so that she
may be made well, and live.' So he went with him.

And a large crowd followed him and pressed in on
him. Now there was a woman who had been suffering
from haemorrhages for twelve years. She had endured
much under many physicians, and had spent all that she
had; and she was no better, but rather grew worse. She
had heard about Jesus, and came up behind him in
the crowd and touched his cloak, for she said, 'If I but
touch his clothes, I will be made well.' Immediately
her haemorrhage stopped; and she felt in her body that
she was healed of her disease. Immediately aware that
power had gone forth from him, Jesus turned about in
the crowd and said, 'Who touched my clothes?' And his
disciples said to him, 'You see the crowd pressing in on
you; how can you say, 'Who touched me?' He looked all
around to see who had done it. But the woman, knowing
what had happened to her, came in fear and trembling,
fell down before him, and told him the whole truth. He
said to her, 'Daughter, your faith has made you well; go
in peace, and be healed of your disease.'

While he was still speaking, some people came
from the leader's house to say, 'Your daughter is dead.

Why trouble the teacher any further?' But overhearing what they said, Jesus said to the leader of the synagogue, 'Do not fear, only believe.' He allowed no one to follow him except Peter, James, and John, the brother of James. When they came to the house of the leader of the synagogue, he saw a commotion, people weeping and wailing loudly. When he had entered, he said to them, 'Why do you make a commotion and weep? The child is not dead but sleeping.' And they laughed at him. Then he put them all outside, and took the child's father and mother and those who were with him, and went in where the child was. [41] He took her by the hand and said to her, 'Talitha cum,' which means, 'Little girl, get up!' And immediately the girl got up and began to walk about (she was twelve years of age). At this they were overcome with amazement. (Mark 5:21-43)

In this episode there are crowds and isolation, community and intimacy. There is desperation and a reaching out. There is compassion and restoration.

The daughter of Jairus is held within the love of a family and within the intergenerational bonds of the wider community who gather at the home. In contrast, the woman with the haemorrhage is isolated from her community, deemed unclean due to her menstrual condition. The expression 'lonely in a crowd' comes to mind, yet just like Jairus' daughter this woman is a unique individual.

Whilst the disciples see and feel an amorphous jostling crowd, Jesus sees individuals and recognises specificity, hence those extraordinary words 'who touched me?' Then comes a moment of encounter marked by compassion and intimacy. Here is a Jewish man not only engaging with a woman but with one considered unclean, and yet just like the man possessed by demons, she is not an 'other'. Furthermore, what began as a reaching out for some sort of transfer of power, becomes a moment of restoration such that new relationships can be lived, not only within the woman's family and community, but most importantly with Jesus Christ himself who movingly calls her 'daughter'. Only a few verses earlier we have heard Jairus use the word 'daughter' – the diminutive of the same word used by Jesus to the woman.

As I look back on my own life, those female familial descriptions of daughter, granddaughter, sister, niece, aunt, and now wife, speak of relationships which have shaped me but have not defined me. They are also relationships I have experienced as love. That does not mean there has been an absence of pain or anger or regret or longing, but it does mean that there has been care, acceptance and a desire for wellbeing.

Time with family was a key part of my sabbatical, not least a special weekend with my parents, siblings and spouses hosted by my sister and brother-in-law at their home on the Isle of Tiree in the Hebrides.

I also had a number of days holidaying with various aunts and uncles, cousins and their children. Conversation around daughters was prominent. My mother is one of four daughters and the bonds between them, and between them and their parents, have significantly shaped our identity as a family and the narrative we share.

During those days in the summer, time was spent looking at old photographs, often trying to identify the place and event at which different family members from different generations were present. For all of us those photos evoked a range of complex emotions, not least a mingling of joy and sadness as we talked not only about our maternal grandparents and the significant role they played in our lives, but also our realisation that in the coming years we will probably see each other more at funerals than parties and weddings.

I remember the day several years ago at a small family gathering when we heard that the child to be adopted as a daughter by one of my cousins and his wife was to be wonderfully named after my grandmother who died many years ago. This naming of her felt deeply significant, and in the summer I enjoyed showing that much loved and precious child photos of her namesake, not least because for her, inhabiting an identity as daughter and sister within a new family has not always been easy.

There were a number of occasions when with family this year I felt once more the pangs of longing to have inhabited the label of mother, and yet I am grateful to have shared a little in the joy and pain of different sisters and daughters both within our family and with god daughters. Over the years I have walked with some of them in their painful issues of separation, divorce, adoption and loss as well as the delight of family life, including joyful weddings and births.

As I imagined the woman in the noisy crowd hearing Jesus call her 'daughter', I found myself thinking about women in prison, often crowded and noisy places.

My relationship with the female estate began on the day I was announced as Bishop of Gloucester. On that memorable day in March 2015 I visited a number of different places within the diocese, travelling with the staff team who I had met for the first time. I will never forget climbing into the minibus to find that someone had tied a pink balloon inside holding the words 'It's a girl'!

The visits that day included an agricultural university, a secondary school, a women's prison and a hospice, before arriving at the cathedral for evensong. In each of these places I met those who are sons and daughters, brothers and sisters and parents, and it is the visits to the prison and hospice that vividly come back to me in relation to this passage in Mark's gospel. Both were places where people spoke poignantly and sometimes with desperation about their own condition and their hopes and fears regarding family members.

The visit that day to HMP Eastwood Park began a special relationship which has led to a deepening of my passion for transformation in the lives of vulnerable women, many of whom would not use the word 'love' as an appropriate description of their relationship experiences. I subsequently took on the national role of Anglican bishop to women's prisons and my encounters with prisoners and staff continue to impact my head and my heart as I live my leadership.

As I stood before the Daniel Cariola painting in Magdala (as referenced in the introduction of this book and seen on the cover) I was struck by the woman's outstretched hand speaking of decision as well as desperation.

If you are a woman caught up in the criminal justice system, taking that decision to reach out for restoration is often far from easy, particularly if your story has been dominated by being 'done to' and in which the outstretched hand towards you has not been one of care and compassion. Of the roughly 4,000 women in prison over 60 per cent have been victims of sexual or domestic abuse, whether as a child or an adult. The majority of women who are at risk of offending or who are given a prison sentence, have complex needs and have lived with multiple disadvantages. More often than not self-esteem is low and vulnerability is high.

As my eyes were drawn to the spark at the place of touch in the Cariola painting, I was reminded of Michelangelo's fresco of the Creation of Adam in the Sistine Chapel. The hand of God is outstretched to the hand of Adam and there is a sense of anticipation of the divine spark giving life.

Cariola's painting also conveys creativity but now it is the touch of the Son of God restoring creation. I am very aware that sometimes my pride slows me down in stretching out my hand to accept God's touch of healing restoration, and often that means having the courage to reach out to another person or respond to their extended hand.

For women in prison (approximately half of whom are serving short, but often repeated sentences, for minor offences), making a choice to reach out for healing and restoration only appears to become a possibility when there is a holistic approach to addressing her issues as her story is heard and the trauma of her life is recognised. While some women are able to engage with such an approach in prison, made possible through trained staff, chaplains and volunteers, the reality is that the needs of most women would probably be better served in their communities.

In recent years I have been inspired by the work of Women's

Centres, and it was a privilege to become President of the Nelson Trust in 2019. I have seen the transformation that is possible when women are offered support and input that recognises them as a whole person. Issues such as addiction are addressed alongside appropriate input regarding areas such as self-esteem, parenting or anger management. There is a recognition and focus on the trauma in the women's lives, and they are able to build relationships of trust in a place of safety.

In that encounter in Mark's gospel when the woman kneels before Jesus and explains her situation, Jesus sees who she is in her entirety, and in his words of peace I hear deep 'shalom' and the widening of the vista of possibility in her life going forward.

For me, it is devastating to see that despite reports and campaigns over the past twelve years or so, there is still no adequate provision of Women's Centres and so much prison sentencing continues to be inappropriate. In all of this, I have appreciated connecting with individuals, charities and organisations committed to campaigning for reform in the whole sphere of female offending.

Towards the end of the episode in chapter 5 of Mark's gospel, restoration is seen again as Jesus raises Jairus' daughter. In the church at Magdala, there is a beautiful mosaic depicting this scene of tenderness, as this time it is Jesus' hand that reaches out.

Once again she is someone of significance and I find myself beginning to feel aggrieved that while Jairus and the male disciples are named by the gospel writer, the woman and the girl are unnamed, and yet they are so deeply acknowledged by Jesus who treats them with dignity and respect.

It seemed serendipitous to me that the United Nations Sustainable Development Goals[18] were adopted by world leaders in the same month as I was inaugurated as Bishop of Gloucester. I continue to explore how I can use who I am more fully to act and speak out for justice, particularly when

---

[18] Goal 5: 'Achieve gender equality and empower all women and girls'.

it comes to the fifth of the SDGs focused on gender equality and the empowerment of women and girls both nationally and internationally.

I certainly recognise many examples of gender stereotyping in my years of growing up, and I also recognise many signs of gender justice which have undoubtedly influenced my commitment to the latter. Although a seemingly trivial example, at quite a young age I asked to join the then 'boys only' church choir and I don't recall meeting with resistance.

As I look back on the relationships and encounters that have shaped me, I recognise that I have been encouraged and enabled to make choices that have been good for my well-being and becoming, and all that began with the love of my parents and my home which was a good place to be.

That parental love and care which I also perceive in Jairus and his wife, has been absent in the lives of numerous children in the world, including many of those women in prison. For some children the pain has come as a result of experiencing separation or loss of a parent who has been their source of love and security. Of course, this is true of many children separated from parents in prison. For other children who suffer, their agony has arisen from neglect or abuse, sometimes masquerading as love. I have been changed and shaped by my own encounters with children lacking the love and care of parents and family, both in my work as a speech and language therapist, in my time in parish ministry, and more recently in my engagement with charities and organisations as a bishop, both locally and internationally.

I see now with even greater clarity that my childhood home was not only a safe place for me, but also a generous place of hospitality for other people. It was not unusual for friends to be in and out of our home, often being invited to stay for meals. Adults living on their own were also frequently invited to join us for meals and our house was a place of intergenerational welcome. I still see this now in my parents' lives, even though they are in their eighth decade.

As I conclude my reflections on those encounters with Jesus in which 'daughter' is prominent, I find myself recalling the hymn 'It is well with my soul'. The rather dated words were written by Horatio Spafford in 1873 as he travelled to meet his wife in England and passed nearby the place where his daughters had drowned at sea. His wife had survived and had sent him a telegram which had simply said 'Saved alone'. I cannot hear that hymn without feeling a lump in my throat.

Spafford was denied the joy experienced by Jairus, and the woman with the haemorrhage knew about the stormy waves of life. And yet in each of these people I see an encounter with Jesus Christ which is about the deep inner place of the soul where true wellness is located. I have personally discovered that human wholeness requires endless touches of loving restoration as we live in relationship with God and neighbour. The two are inseparable as we live in the love of divine and human connectedness, sons and daughters of God and sisters and brothers of one another. In this, the kingdom of God is proclaimed.

Prayer

Jesus, like a mother you gather your people to you;
you are gentle with us as a mother with her children.

Often you weep over our sins and our pride,
tenderly you draw us from hatred and judgement.

You comfort us in sorrow and bind up our wounds,
in sickness you nurse us, and with pure milk you feed us.

Jesus, by your dying we are born to new life;
by your anguish and labour we come forth in joy.

Despair turns to hope through your sweet goodness;
through your gentleness we find comfort in fear.

Your warmth gives life to the dead,
your touch makes sinners righteous.

BELOVED DAUGHTERS

Lord Jesus, in your mercy heal us;
in your love and tenderness remake us.

In your compassion bring grace and forgiveness,
for the beauty of heaven may your love prepare us.

A song of Anselm of Canterbury (*Common Worship* daily
prayer material, © The Archbishops' Council, 2005)

NOTES

Chapter 8

IDENTITY

[Jesus] came to a Samaritan city called Sychar … Jacob's well was there, and Jesus, tired out by his journey, was sitting by the well. It was about noon.

A Samaritan woman came to draw water, and Jesus said to her, 'Give me a drink'. (His disciples had gone to the city to buy food.) The Samaritan woman said to him, 'How is it that you, a Jew, ask a drink of me, a woman of Samaria?' (Jews do not share things in common with Samaritans.) Jesus answered her, 'If you knew the gift of God, and who it is that is saying to you, "Give me a drink", you would have asked him, and he would have given you living water.' The woman said to him, 'Sir, you have no bucket, and the well is deep. Where do you get that living water? Are you greater than our ancestor Jacob, who gave us the well, and with his sons and his flocks drank from it?' Jesus said to her, 'Everyone who drinks of this water will be thirsty again, but those who drink of the water that I will give them will never be thirsty. The water that I will give will become in them a spring of water gushing up to eternal life.' The woman said to him, 'Sir, give me this water, so that I may never be thirsty or have to keep coming here to draw water.'

Jesus said to her, 'Go, call your husband, and come back.' The woman answered him, 'I have no husband.' Jesus said to her, 'You are right in saying, "I have no husband"; for you have had five husbands, and the one you have now is not your husband. What you have said is true!' …

The woman said to him, 'I know that Messiah is coming' (who is called Christ). 'When he comes, he will proclaim all things to us.' Jesus said to her, 'I am he, the one who is speaking to you.'...

Just then his disciples came. They were astonished that he was speaking with a woman, but no one said, 'What do you want?' or, 'Why are you speaking with her?' Then the woman left her water jar and went back to the city. She said to the people, 'Come and see a man who told me everything I have ever done! He cannot be the Messiah, can he?' They left the city and were on their way to him ...

Many Samaritans from that city believed in him because of the woman's testimony, 'He told me everything I have ever done.' So when the Samaritans came to him, they asked him to stay with them; and he stayed there two days. And many more believed because of his word. They said to the woman, 'It is no longer because of what you said that we believe, for we have heard for ourselves, and we know that this is truly the Saviour of the world.' (John 4:5-42)

I mentioned in chapter 3 how at my inauguration as Bishop of Gloucester I was met by a young person, not at a well but at a font, as I identified myself as 'Rachel, a pilgrim and servant of Jesus...'.

Identity is a major topic for study and discussion in many spheres of life including different fields of research and therapeutic practice. Whether the topic is gender identity or what it means to be human amid the development of Artificial Intelligence, questions around identity are very much part of our twenty-first-century landscape and I have commented in chapter 2 on my work around Liedentity.

In the above passage from John's gospel, we encounter a woman who is hiding. If there had been social media at that time, we can begin to imagine what might have been posted about her and how she might have felt.

Unlike Jesus we don't know her full story, but we know that she comes to a well to draw water in the heat of the midday sun. That was usually a task for the cool of the morning or the evening so we begin to sense the gravity of this woman's desire not to encounter other people at a place where there would be conversation and interaction.

Yet an encounter does take place – an encounter with Jesus Christ. What unfolds is an extraordinary conversation between a man and a woman, which was in itself something rather counter cultural at that time. Even more shocking is the realisation that the man is Jewish and the woman is a Samaritan thus representing two communities who loathed each other.

In this highly unusual place of encounter, uncomfortable truth is named but so too is a new expression of freedom.

Jesus names some truth regarding the woman's series of husbands and the man she now lives with, who is not her husband. There is clearly a deeper story beneath the headlines and we are not privy to that, but what we do recognise is the woman's shame. It's implicit in her 'hiding'.

A number of years ago I watched a powerful TED talk by Dr Brené Brown, a research professor at the University of Houston. She was speaking about some research she had undertaken on vulnerability and how she discovered the thing called shame. She describes it as the 'fear of disconnection' focused on our fear that we are not good enough and that if other people knew about particular things in our lives then they would not see us as 'worthy of connection'.

In her research Brené Brown discovered that what kills shame is acceptance and complete love. Shame cannot survive if we can honestly share our story with someone who responds with empathy. I believe this is what we are beginning to see in this encounter between Jesus and the woman at well. God sees us as we are and does not withdraw.

Although we might find some of the discourse around belief, water and truth a little perplexing, we do hear Jesus clearly speaking words of life and hope.

There is so much we don't discover about this encounter and

what emerged from it, but we do know that something within the woman changed and she became a catalyst for community transformation and discovery.

From someone trying to stay hidden there emerges a woman who engages with the community in the telling of her encounter. Furthermore, something within her led the people of the community not to dismiss her but to go and see for themselves and 'many believed because of the woman's testimony'. Jesus then stays with the Samaritan community for two days.

Here is discovery in relationship and the emergence of a plethora of questions and challenges for the woman and the community around both their identity and that of Jesus.

This story is not one that dwells on shame, but rather shines a light on being known. The truth that there is hope and the possibility of restoration which impacts relationship and community is something I have already reflected on in the previous chapter of this book. As with other gospel encounters, the episode with the Samaritan woman reminds us that we each have a story to tell. The little book at primary school in which I wrote that I wanted to be an author, also included the hope that I would be married with two children and a cat and live in Sussex. As an aside, I suspect the desire to live in Sussex came from the fact that it is where my maternal grandparents lived and was a place of happy holidays, but I'm not sure about the cat as I have always shown a level of indifference towards them. However, that little book of 'My Life' was clearly proving not to be prophetic, and at the age of thirty I found myself at theological college, unmarried and preparing for ordination in a church which as yet had not taken the decision to ordain women to the priesthood. It is true that I was a fairly confident young woman, but that didn't mean life was pain-free or that I didn't frequently ache with longing to have more than a platonic friendship with a man. Furthermore, Wycliffe Hall was a theological college at which a large percentage of students and staff had strong views about the role of women in the Church and held to a theology of male headship, resulting in a view that women should not preach or be ordained as priests and definitely should not be church leaders.

As I look back, I more deeply appreciate how painful life must often have been for Vera Sinton, the pastoral theology tutor who was an ordained deacon. The wonderful connection for me was that Vera had been the deaconess at my church in Broxbourne and as a single woman she had often joined us for family meals in our home. She had been a person of wisdom, prayer and care, particularly in my teens.

I recall one particular morning in the chapel at Wycliffe when one of the staff had been teaching on the early chapters in Genesis. The implication in his words was that the fulfilment of women came through marriage and motherhood. A few of us who were neither married nor mothers expressed anger, hurt and bewilderment and gathered together to reflect on what this all meant with regards to our identity and calling as we continued to live in community at Wycliffe. It was often painful, but I am grateful that amid an environment where there were such strong opposing views there were also a substantial number of people committed to honest conversation and staying in relationship. It was good preparation for the path ahead, not only in all the synodical discussions and decision-making around women in the episcopate, but also in my ministry as an archdeacon in London and now as a bishop. I have sought to inhabit the role to which I have been called with appropriate authority while staying in good relationship with those who remain unable to accept the ministry of female priests and bishops.

As to the gift of marriage, meeting Guy in my forties was an immeasurable blessing and I am daily thankful for the priceless gift of him in my life and for the ways our relationship continues to change me. My years as a single woman were also gift, but in a different way as I grew in who I am.

In all of this there have been significant shifts in my identity in terms of how I perceive myself and am perceived, perhaps most memorably in the first few weeks after our wedding. In the space of six weeks I moved from being a single vicar in the East End of London with the title Reverend and the surname Montgomery, to being a married Archdeacon in a part of London I did not know and bearing the strange title of The Venerable with a new surname of Treweek. I had underestimated how discombobulating all this change would be, coming all at once, and on one particular day when I was feeling tired and inept at living the new territory of being an archdeacon and was still trying to work out the geography of North West London, I decided that the title 'Venerable' would be better recast as 'Vulnerable'. I also recognised the need to give some time to exploring new depths of what it meant for my identity to be in Christ. While it might be a familiar Christian phrase, it requires serious heart work and a rejection of glib answers:

> Your old life is dead. Your new life, which is your *real* life—even though invisible to spectators—is with Christ in God. *He* is your life. When Christ (your real life, remember) shows up again on this earth, you'll show up, too—the real you, the glorious you. Meanwhile, be content with obscurity, like Christ.[19]

In the encounter between the woman and Jesus at the well, I see the woman not only as someone with her own story engaged in an intimate encounter with Jesus, I also see someone who as a woman and as a Samaritan was representing some important things that were being revealed regarding Christ's radical engagement with individuals and communities in his revelation of God's transforming work of complete reconciliation.

I know that in my calling to be Rachel I was called to be Bishop of Gloucester, and yet as the first female diocesan bishop it was sometimes awkward in the very early days to embody a role which was not only about me but also about a bigger narrative.

---

[19] Colossians 3:3-4 *The Message*.

When someone is appointed as a diocesan bishop the election of the new bishop has to be confirmed in an ancient legal event in which sacred worship and almost theatrical legal processes are woven together. I have heard it light-heartedly described as something akin to a Gilbert and Sullivan operetta.

When it came to my Confirmation of Election at St Mary-le-Bow in the City of London it was the first time that the bishop in question was a woman, but I don't think I had fully appreciated the reality of its place in history. I was simply trying to keep up with all the steps in the process to taking up my post in the Diocese of Gloucester.

St Mary-le-Bow was full and when the applause broke out at the end of the service it seemed to go on almost interminably. I stood there feeling overwhelmed and awkward wondering how I could adopt a bodily posture which conveyed something of my recognition that whilst amid the clapping there was affirmation of me as Rachel, it was primarily about this longed-for moment and what it said about women, the Church and God's purposes. I was, and remain, very aware of all those who prayed, debated and campaigned over many years for this moment to be realised and I needed to embrace that in what I represented.

There have been a number of other occasions since then when I have felt that same tension between personal affirmation on the one hand, and on the other hand appropriately holding a space for other people to celebrate something significant in the history of the Church as the breaking in of God's kingdom continues. These occasions notably included my consecration at Canterbury Cathedral alongside Sarah Mullally and my introduction to the House of Lords as the first female Lords Spiritual, which I write about later in this book.

Prayer

Almighty God,

who wonderfully created us in your own image

and yet more wonderfully restored us through your Son
Jesus Christ:

grant that, as he came to share in our humanity, so we
may share the life of his divinity;

who is alive and reigns with you, in the unity of the Holy
Spirit,

one God, now and for ever

(Collect from *Common Worship*, © The Archbishops'
Council of the Church of England)

NOTES

Chapter 9

THE RHYTHM OF GOD

Now as they went on their way, Jesus entered a certain village, where a woman named Martha welcomed him into her home. She had a sister named Mary, who sat at the Lord's feet and listened to what he was saying. But Martha was distracted by her many tasks; so she came to him and asked, 'Lord, do you not care that my sister has left me to do all the work by myself? Tell her then to help me.' But the Lord answered her, 'Martha, Martha, you are worried and distracted by many things; there is need of only one thing. Mary has chosen the better part, which will not be taken away from her.' (Luke 10:38 – 42)

Here is yet another encounter between Jesus and someone called Mary – this time the sister of Martha and Lazarus – siblings who were friends of Jesus and lived in Bethany.

Mary knew the one thing and just as with Mary the Mother of Jesus, it began in a place of dependence. It wasn't that labour was not valued by Jesus (and probably needed to occupy further hours that same day), but rather it was about understanding the present moment.

Sometimes when I hear people talking about 'doing' and 'being' it is as if they are at odds with one another, and sometimes the 'being' is perceived as a more holy state, often equated with prayerful stillness. The reality is that in our human being there will be both times of stillness and times of activity, just as we see in Jesus' earthly ministry. What matters is the place from which they emerge and how we daily live the rhythm of God. In the case of Mary and Martha there was an appropriate time for domestic tasks, but the immediate moment was to sit at Jesus' feet and learn from him.

I loathe hearing or reading words directed at me with great frequency, which go something along the lines of 'I know how busy you are ...'. I flinch when I hear words such as this because I do not want to be known as 'busy'. Personally, I equate busyness with a sense of rushing and a propensity to see 'more' as good. I believe busyness is rooted in human striving and can sometimes be motivated by the need to achieve and succeed, or to be needed and valued. Busyness is about 'too much' and a sense of trying to achieve more than time will allow, and perhaps I have a visceral reaction to the word because it touches on something that I know is sometimes true in my life.

Sometimes when I am endeavouring to action my 'to do' list, gain clarity on required agenda items, attend fully to pastoral encounters, reflect on possible solutions to perceived pressing problems, and engage with preparation for sermons and worship and issues in the public square, I can to my abhorrence, find that I am busy, and such days are rarely ones of which I am proud. I find myself feeling rushed as I strive in my own strength, and fail to live in each present moment. Such days feel very different from those days that are 'full'. On full days the diary might appear no different from the days when I am busy but importantly there is a strong sense of each activity or task having its right time and place. I know myself intentionally rooted in God as I move from one thing to another with a strong sense of God's rhythm. It is likely that I have let go and cried dependence on God at the start of the day as I have acknowledged 'The night has passed, and the day lies open before us'.[20]

I am reminded of Jesus' story of the wise and foolish builder.[21] We frequently sang the children's song about it on

---

[20] Church of England *Common Worship*, Order for Morning Prayer, © Archbishops' Council.
[21] Matthew 7:24-27.

that beach in Criccieth and I loved the loud clap we all made as we sang the final line: 'And the house on the sand fell flat.' Yet it's only in more recent years that I've pondered on the fact that the house built on rock and the house built on sand might have looked identical. In theory the occupants of both could have named them as good places to inhabit, and both properties could have been equally attractive to passers-by. Potentially the house built on the sand might even have been more admired than the house on the rock. The foundations could not be seen and therein lies the difference.

Psalm 127:1-2
Unless the LORD builds the house,
those who build it labour in vain.
Unless the LORD guards the city,
the guard keeps watch in vain.
It is in vain that you rise up early
and go late to rest,
eating the bread of anxious toil;
for he gives sleep to his beloved.

For me, dependency on God is not a letting go in tiredness at the end of the day or letting go only when things are finished. It is a starting place and a mode of being and becoming, so even when a day is full with one thing after another, there will be a sense of being present to each task and person, and attention to see and smell and hear each thing around me. Sadly, when I have not lived such dependence and let God set the rhythm whether in the planning or the living of that day, I frequently experience a sense of rushing and like Martha I often fail to choose the one right thing.

Unfortunately, we live in a culture in which busyness is often equated with importance or significance. Sometimes people boast of their busyness as if it increases their worthiness, or even their holiness. Too often I hear people in worshipping communities commended for their busyness, and those listening soon add their agreement to the accolade and so it is that we continue to perpetuate a dangerous myth about busyness and personal value. I think that Martha was living something of that and is uncomfortably challenged in her encounter with Jesus Christ in her home.

The truth is that busy people are loved and valued simply because they are 'fearfully and wonderfully made' in the image of God.[22] More and more activity won't make us more loved or significant in the eyes of God.

Whilst I was in Galilee I was glad to visit the Church of the Multiplication of the Loaves and Fishes at Tabgha, close to the Church of the Primacy of St Peter to which I refer in chapter 12.

The existing Church of the Multiplication was built on the site of a fourth-century church, with beautiful Byzantine mosaics on the floor, the most famous of which depicts two fish with a basket of loaves between them. I had seen this image before in numerous pictures and vibrant blue pottery so I was grateful to finally see it for myself.

Irrespective of whether or not the site of the church, and more specifically the altar, is actually the site where the miracle took place, the church has been a place of prayer and reflection for hundreds of years and bears witness to the narrative of the feeding of the five thousand. That episode in Jesus' ministry (told in all four of the Gospels) is one I frequently bring to mind when my inner resources are at a low ebb or when I have felt my time so squeezed that I have not been sure how I will fulfil all that is necessary and critical within a particular timeframe.

In the telling of the feeding of the five thousand, it is clear that there is something to be done. People who are tired and hungry need food, and Jesus looks for a solution. At this point there is much that could be surmised and discussed regarding the picnic. Is this really the only food available, and how significant is it that the food belongs to a child, and what exactly is the symbolism of the twelve baskets of leftovers gathered up? Yet what strikes me repeatedly in this story is something extremely

---

[22]   Psalm 139:14.

simple: Jesus took the little that was available and gave thanks to God. There was then more than enough to go round.

There was trust in the offering of the little and there was thanksgiving to God.

Sometimes I think of that tiny picnic when I am anxious that who I am or what I have is not enough. Sometimes that feeling of 'not enough' is about time or energy or ideas. Sometimes it is about my own feelings of inadequacy. Yet, when I can remember that picnic I am able to offer God the little I have, knowing in my head that there is enough to be and do what is needed. What is required is an offering of the little with thankfulness and a trusting heart.

However I also know that it is foolish and arrogant if in offering God my little I do so with the expectation that God then has to make it possible for me to accomplish everything I perceive as necessary as reflected in my 'To do list'. That is about me adopting the place of control and expecting God to work some magic at my behest. Such a position is very different from the wisdom of offering God what I have with thanksgiving as I endeavour to do the one right thing in each present moment.

It is interesting that Mary sitting at Jesus' feet echoes some verses a couple of chapters earlier in Luke's gospel in the same episode that is told in Mark chapter 5 and which I have written about in chapter 6 of this book. After Jesus has cast out the demons from the man in the country of the Gerasenes, Luke tells how the people find him sitting at the feet of Jesus.[23] It is from this place that Jesus sends him away to tell people of what God has done for him. There is to be purposeful activity but it begins in a place of dependency at the feet of Jesus, just as with Mary.

In my relationship with God and my evolving experience of leadership, the issue of giving attention to the locus of control is a recurring theme. In recent years there has been something of an air of criticism regarding what some have perceived to be

[23] Luke 8:35.

a preponderance of so called management-speak when talking about the Church's mission and ministry, yet for me the issue is not one of language and words but rather the need to focus on motivation. In terms of direction, vision and strategy there is no reticence in the ministry of Christ to call people to action. Prior to this encounter in the home of Mary and Martha as told by Luke, we hear of Jesus sending out the seventy two who are given clear instructions and told to 'go'. This is then followed by Jesus telling the parable of the Good Samaritan in response to a question. That episode ends with Jesus' words, 'go and do likewise'.

In the Gospels we have a number of occasions where Jesus is clear about the need for action. Sometimes he has withdrawn to a quiet place but is found by his disciples or the crowds and soon engages with them once again. This is true of the narrative in the verses preceding the feeding of the five thousand as told by Matthew, Mark and Luke. Yet in the activity, attention always needs to be given to the motivation and the place from which plans and activity emerge.

I want to participate in the godly urgency I hear in Christ's imperative to join in with the breaking in of the kingdom of God, but I find anxious talk of burning platforms or threatening talk of metaphorical melting icebergs decidedly enervating when it comes to the mission of the Church.

God's kingdom is unshakeable. Nothing can undo the resurrection. God is not a fragile God who needs my protection. I know that my 'yes' of participation is not to be half-hearted, but sometimes it seems as if Christ's Church is wanting to shoulder a responsibility of saving God rather than participating in the transforming work of God who has already secured our salvation.

When our strategies and initiatives give us security such that we feel as if we are now in control, then I believe there is a need for challenge. Likewise, when prayer is not the spring from which activity bubbles forth then we need to pause.

And yet even as I voice that criticism I am unnerved by how easy it is to direct my gaze towards other people and take my eyes off my own interior landscape. So it is that I find myself returning to the words and images of Psalm 131:

> O LORD, my heart is not lifted up,
> my eyes are not raised too high;
> I do not occupy myself with things
> too great and too marvellous for me.
> But I have calmed and quieted my soul,
> like a weaned child with its mother;
> my soul is like the weaned child that is with me.
> O Israel, hope in the LORD
> from this time on and for evermore.

Prayer

> Leave me alone with God as much as may be.
> As the tide draws the waters close in upon the shore,
> Make me an island, set apart,
> alone with you, God, holy to you.
>
> Then with the turning of the tide
> prepare me to carry your presence to the busy world
>   beyond,
> the world that rushes in on me
> till the waters come again and fold me back to you.

Aidan of Lindisfarne

NOTES

Chapter 10

INSIDE OUT

[Jesus] entered Jericho and was passing through it. A man was there named Zacchaeus; he was a chief tax collector and was rich. He was trying to see who Jesus was, but on account of the crowd he could not, because he was short in stature. So he ran ahead and climbed a sycamore tree to see him, because he was going to pass that way. When Jesus came to the place, he looked up and said to him, 'Zacchaeus, hurry and come down; for I must stay at your house today.' So he hurried down and was happy to welcome him. All who saw it began to grumble and said, 'He has gone to be the guest of one who is a sinner.' Zacchaeus stood there and said to the Lord, 'Look, half of my possessions, Lord, I will give to the poor; and if I have defrauded anyone of anything, I will pay back four times as much.' Then Jesus said to him, 'Today salvation has come to this house, because he too is a son of Abraham. For the Son of Man came to seek out and to save the lost.' (Luke 19:1-10)

In chapter 2 I wrote about the Liedentity campaign launched in 2016. It enabled me to add my voice to the truth that human value is not about appearance and that happiness is not about individualism.

While Liedentity has primarily focussed on young people, the issue for me has always been more extensive than that and encompasses the way we make value judgements based on what we see in people's appearance. That might be to do with orthodontics, physical disabilities or conditions which affect parts of the body such as skin or hair. I recall how very early on in the campaign I received some heart-wrenching correspondence from a mother who spoke of her son's death by suicide following the bullying he attributed to his appearance as someone with cerebral palsy.

However, one of the prime reasons for Liedentity is a desire to be involved with issues that concern young people. If I genuinely want to engage with young people in a way that is truly about their flourishing, then I need to be listening, always being aware that 'young people' are not a group of 'others' and they are no more a homogenous group than old people or middle aged people, or indeed tax collectors.

This is about unique individuals with a range of hopes and fears lived out within their individual stories and contexts, recognising that we only truly go on becoming as we live in relationship. On my sabbatical visit to South Africa in 2019 I visited the Desmond and Leah Tutu Legacy Foundation and was reminded once more of Archbishop Desmond Tutu's theological reflections around the African concept of Ubuntu. It is not an easy word to translate but Tutu has described it as 'I am because we are.' It is about the inextricable connection between human beings who are precious individuals, but interdependent.

Zacchaeus is a unique individual with a name and a story, and in this short episode in Luke's gospel we see him moving from a place of dislocated relationship to a place of new possibility and connection.

We know that Zacchaeus was rich and a chief tax collector but beyond that we are not told anything about his life story and who he really is. We primarily see him through the eyes of those around him who grumble and label him a sinner because in that context a tax collector such as Zacchaeus would have been seen as dishonest. In relation to the passage, it is worth noting that Jews looked on any house where a tax collector entered as unclean.

In chapter 2, I drew attention to the looking and seeing of the heart as well as that of the eyes, and once more looking and seeing are strong components in this encounter.

We know that Zacchaeus wanted to see Jesus and because of his height he needed to climb a tree. On the surface we read this 'seeing' as something physical and practical, yet Zacchaeus's desire to see Jesus is something much deeper than an immediate viewing with the eyes. I believe there was a desire in Zacchaeus to know who Jesus was and to see in a way which was about understanding.

Amazingly, Jesus *sees* Zacchaeus. Again, this is not simply a physical noticing as Jesus looks up to the tree, but rather in this looking there is a deep seeing regarding all that Zacchaeus is, his story and the inner landscape of his heart. It is not unlike the encounter with the Samaritan woman at the well. Jesus sees and knows and in inviting himself to Zacchaeus' house Jesus is saying something significant about the possibility of Zacchaeus and all people finding their home in God.

I do not believe it is a coincidence that once Zacchaeus has been seen by Jesus he refers to Jesus as Lord. Zacchaeus has begun to see not only with his eyes as he peered at Jesus from the branches of a tree, but also with his heart. This looking and seeing leads to inner transformation and we glimpse Zacchaeus-the-individual being transformed in his relationship not only with money but also in relation to God and neighbour.

As I discuss seeing and appearance in my Liedentity work with young people I repeatedly use the phrase 'inside out'. I like it because it is often used in everyday life to draw attention to something that's not quite as it should be, for example a piece of clothing that is incorrectly being worn inside out. The phrase echoes the truth that we are far from perfect but it also proclaims the truth that who we are begins on the inside and radiates out. We need to look and see beyond the surface appearance of ourselves and other people.

It gladdened my heart to discover *The Message* translation of Psalm 139:

Oh yes, you shaped me first inside, then out;
you formed me in my mother's womb.[24]

This message of 'inside out' is also found in the Apostle Paul's letters to the Christians in Corinth. He penned some beautiful words about Christians being ordinary clay jars, but with God's treasure within them.[25]

Middle Eastern pottery jars were very breakable – cracks easily appeared and the clay was often flawed, and there is evidence to suggest that these jars were used as lanterns. The flame lit within them would have shone most visibly through the cracks and holes and thin places.

Those words of Paul have been poignant for me in my life. However physically flawed I might feel, and however crushed or struck down or perplexed I might feel at times, I can remind myself that God has put Christ's light within me, and I do believe that it can shine from the inside out.

Sometimes I think we are a little fearful of being open to that light with which God longs to fill us because we are so aware of the cracks and flaws and those deep and secret places which we wish to stay hidden.

As I speak to other people about the Liedentity message of 'inside out' and not 'outside in' I need to hear it myself. I am not immune from failing to remember that who I am and who I am becoming begins on the *inside*, deep within me, and not on the outside.

There are times when I have gathered with other people in positions of leadership, not least bishops, and have felt deeply inadequate in my presence and contribution. Sometimes this resonates with what has become known as 'impostor syndrome', which apparently is not uncommon among those in positions of leadership. It is characterised by self-doubt and a fear of being revealed as a fraud who should not be occupying the position they are in.

[24] Psalm 139:13-15, *The Message.*
[25] 2 Corinthians 4:7-11.

I remember feeling this acutely on 26 October 2015 when I was introduced to the House of Lords. Following the 2014 legislation allowing for women and men to be consecrated as bishops, the Lords Spiritual (Women) Act 2015 soon came into force. The act stipulates that for ten years after the Act came into operation, a vacancy in the Lords Spiritual (due to the retirement of a bishop) will be filled by the longest serving female diocesan bishop not yet in the House of Lords. If there is no such woman then the place will be filled as usual by the longest serving male diocesan bishop.

Tim Stevens had retired as Bishop of Leicester in the summer of 2015 so it meant that I was to be introduced when parliament reconvened in the autumn. Unlike most Lords Spiritual who have usually been bishops for a while before entering the House of Lords, I had only been consecrated in July 2015 and had my inauguration service at Gloucester Cathedral in late September. Everything was very new and the learning curve steep, so now to be faced with another 'first' in the spotlight of the media was a little daunting, particularly as Politics with a capital 'P' had never really occupied much space on the canvas of my life. The opportunity to use my voice and insights for the well-being of people and place was (and is) an unexpected privilege but I had never imagined myself walking the corridors of Westminster.

The issue that most interested the media was the fact that I had returned my writ of summons. The papers made it sound as if I had sent it back in a fit of pique whereas the returned writ had been accompanied by a simple question, politely asked, and concerned the fact that the summons referred to me as 'Right Reverend Father in God'. The writ was duly changed to read 'Right Reverend' and since then the words of 'Father in God' have been omitted from all writs for men and women.

After the short ceremony of introduction, at which I was accompanied by the Archbishop of Canterbury, Justin Welby, and the then Bishop of London, Richard Chartres, there was a short outbreak of quiet applause which I soon learned was not the usual custom in the Lords, but the historic moment provoked the momentary break with tradition.

As I took my seat on the red benches I smiled confidently on the outside but on the inside I had what I can only describe as an attack of imposter syndrome.

In such situations I find strength in deliberately bringing to mind what has become for me a much-loved episode in the first Book of Samuel which focuses on God's affirmation and clear calling. The prophet Samuel is sent to the home of Jesse to identify one of his sons to succeed Saul as king of Israel (1 Samuel 16:1-13). Samuel quickly forms an impression of Jesse's sons by looking at their physical appearance but he is strongly reminded that God looks not on the outward presentation but at the heart. It is thus the unlikely David, the youngest son looking after the sheep, who is anointed as king. For me the story has some resonances with the fairy-tale story of Cinderella and I now often incorporate it in my Liedentity work in schools and it is featured in the Messy Church session developed as part of that campaign.[26]

In Jesus' encounter with Zacchaeus, Jesus sees his potential, and as Zacchaeus is transformed from the inside out, a yearning to serve God and neighbour is ignited.

I am reminded that authentic servanthood after the pattern of Jesus Christ is rooted in a desire to go on discovering who we are wherever we find ourselves. Perhaps this is most clearly shown in John's gospel chapter 13 in which we are drawn into the scene of Jesus washing the feet of his disciples. It is the Passover supper the night before Jesus is crucified, and we hear him implore his disciples to serve one another. Sadly, I have seen too often how this has led Christians to opt for the doormat pattern of Christian service which is often more about feeding a craving for affirmation or a deep desire to be needed. Yet, Jesus' servanthood is very different. In verse 3 of John 13 we read that 'Jesus, knowing that the Father had given all things into his hands, and that he had come from God and was going to God, got up from the table.'

---

[26] 'The Real Me': Messy Church Bible Reading Fellowship.

Jesus knows who he is and knows his calling, and it is from that place that he chooses to get up from the table – stand up tall – and then chooses to kneel. It is only when we have a sense of who we are and God's generous love for us which can never be earned, that we are able to stand up and choose to kneel.

In the story of Zacchaeus as told by Luke, I see someone who is beginning to see new possibilities and discovering who he can be as he begins to see who Jesus is.

The response to that invitation to find our identity in Christ is one of life-long exploration. I believe that both Zacchaeus and the Samaritan woman began to discover that when they met Jesus and began to truly see from the inside out. I am Rachel continually being shaped from the inside out as I live my life within a network of relationships and endless encounter, and go on discovering more of who I am in Christ amid the rhythm and places of life, of which the red benches is merely one.

Prayer

Take this moment, sign and space;
Take my friends around;
 Here among us make the place
Where your love is found.

Take the time to call my name,
Take the time to mend
Who I am and what I've been,
All I've failed to tend.

 Take the tiredness of my days,
Take my past regret,
Letting your forgiveness touch
All I can't forget

Take the little child in me
Scared of growing old;
Help me here to find my worth
Made in God's own mould.

INSIDE OUT

Take my talents, take my skills,
Take what's yet to be;
Let my life be yours, and yet
Let it still be me.

John L. Bell

Chapter 11

IF ONLY

Now a certain man was ill, Lazarus of Bethany, the village of Mary and her sister Martha.

⋯ When Jesus arrived, he found that Lazarus had already been in the tomb four days. Now Bethany was near Jerusalem, some two miles away, and many of the Jews had come to Martha and Mary to console them about their brother. When Martha heard that Jesus was coming, she went and met him, while Mary stayed at home. Martha said to Jesus, 'Lord, if you had been here, my brother would not have died. But even now I know that God will give you whatever you ask of him.' Jesus said to her, 'Your brother will rise again.'

⋯ Now Jesus had not yet come to the village, but was still at the place where Martha had met him. The Jews who were with her in the house, consoling her, saw Mary get up quickly and go out. They followed her because they thought that she was going to the tomb to weep there. When Mary came where Jesus was and saw him, she knelt at his feet and said to him, 'Lord, if you had been here, my brother would not have died.' ....
(John 11:1-44)

It was the day after the opening ceremony of the London Olympic Games in 2012. It had been a late night on the Friday as I had stayed up to watch the opening extravaganza but I arose early to meet a good friend at the Members' Cafe at Tate Modern, just across the Millennium Bridge near our home in the City of London. There was a palpable sense of camaraderie as people passed one another, and all the fear mongering of the previous months with warnings about people not being able to cross roads or access supermarkets seemed to be rapidly dissipating. People were greeting each other that morning and buildings and pavements were adorned with flowers and flags. I felt a sense of excited anticipation regarding the coming days in London and life felt good.

Soon after I arrived back home on that Saturday the phone rang. It was my sister-in-law, who I knew was on holiday. In a matter of seconds my serenity was shattered.

At that moment my brother was undergoing surgery in Portugal as he had become very ill and a tumour had been found in his bowel. It was very serious.

The phone call finished and I was flooded with a mix of emotions – utter shock, fear and concern, not only for my brother but also for my sister-in-law on her own abroad, and for my nephews and nieces who would be receiving this news.

I went out onto the landing outside my upstairs study and cried out loud – almost a wail – pleading with God, as I inhabited another sister and brother scenario: Mary and Martha at the tomb of Lazarus. I cried out to God and prayed that as Jesus brought Lazarus back to life from the tomb, so God might heal my brother whom I loved. As I stood on that landing I cried out for the outstretched hand of Christ to touch not a tomb but an operating theatre somewhere in Portugal.

That was more than seven years ago and my brother is alive and well. Yet, even more amazing than my brother's recovery was the resurrection of Lazarus, powerfully revealing resurrection and transformation at the heart of the gospel, and even then pointing to the life-changing resurrection of Jesus Christ. Of course one day earthly death will come to my brother just as it eventually did to Lazarus, but in the present moments of this biblical encounter and my personal story there is joyful resolution. It is not always that way and so often the words of 'if only' are articulated through people's tears and longing, sometimes imbued with resentment or regret.

And it is these words of 'if only' which stood out for me as I recently reflected on this episode of Lazarus's death and resurrection.

Martha, and then Mary express that very human sense of regret and deep disappointment, and in their words of 'if only' there is a recognition that things could have unfolded another way. They had both longed for things to be different.

I find it painfully easy to get in touch with all those thoughts and emotions held in that phrase 'if only' and I know I don't do disappointment well.

I remember the first time I was overwhelmed by disappointment. Once again the story involved a pantomime. As a child there was the annual family post-Christmas trip to the local amateur dramatics pantomime in Hertford. It was always the thing on the horizon to look forward to, even when the excitement of Christmas had passed. I loved it because a story came alive in colour and movement and music. It was funny with energetic audience participation and for some reason there always seemed to be Quality Street chocolates to enjoy.

This particular year it snowed heavily. That had been exciting until my mum sat me on her knee and told me we couldn't get to the pantomime that evening because we wouldn't be able to drive the few miles through the snow, not least because one of the hills was impassable. I sobbed and then wailed with frustration. Why couldn't we find a way and why couldn't my parents and grandparents just make it happen – after all they were the grown-ups? And why couldn't we even try? If only things could be different but I was powerless to change the situation.

There have been a number of times in my life since then when my disappointment has taken me straight back to those intense emotions I first experienced in that scene with my mother and granddad trying to explain, but to no avail. I had imagined the shape of life to be one thing and it turned out to be another and I could do nothing to change it. 'If only.' This is not how I wanted things to be.

I have felt like that when exam grades weren't quite what I had expected. I felt like that at the ending of relationships in my twenties and thirties. I felt like it when a major funding application process for the redevelopment of the church crypt in Bethnal Green fell at the last hurdle. I have felt it when I've had to accept that particular posts were not to be.

I've learned that tears and prayers of longing will not always take me to the place I want to be, but I have also discovered that in my impotence to bring about the change for which I long there can be a peace which leads to new life if I dare to let the disappointment die.

I have longed for that in the lives of others too. In my years so far as a Bishop, some of my most acute times of pain have come from my interaction with those who have objected to people or situations and have been unable to let go and move to a place of healing or reconciliation. I have watched with deep sadness and frustration as people have clung to a repeated rendition of 'if only', which seems to have both a paralysing and necrotic effect in their lives.

In my own life there are of course things I don't understand and I can still see the scars even if the wounds have healed. There are also the gifts that have come that I was not able to even glimpse on the horizon at certain times of 'if only'. Back in my early thirties, I never knew the priceless treasure of my husband Guy awaited me, and I certainly couldn't envisage discovering motherhood in the nurture of people in a very different way from the parenthood I had hoped would come.

Of course, my personal disappointments are mere specks on a worldwide canvas marked by the longings of people and nations whether it be the emaciated mother cradling her child dying of starvation, or those living with past or present injustice and abuse, or people fearfully anticipating the next bomb or brutal attack. There are so many words of 'if only' whispered or screamed across our world as people add their tears and cries to the groaning of creation and longing for shalom when one day all shall be well and there will be no more dying or crying or death and God will wipe every tear from our eyes.[27]

As I reflect on various international visits to different parts of Africa and India visiting partner dioceses as well as trips in 2019 to Egypt and Srebrenica, so many encounters come to mind in which 'if only' is writ large. However, the story I have found myself recalling so vividly in relation to this episode from John's gospel, is an encounter with a mother in Soweto in 2002. I was visiting the Revd Thato Molipa, at that time the priest at Holy Cross, Orlando West.

Due to my interest in South Africa following my pre-ordination placement in 1994, I was introduced to Thato when he visited Islington in 1995. I have stayed in touch with him and his family ever since and visited on several occasions. I was delighted that he and his daughter attended my consecration in Canterbury in 2015.

On my visit in 2002 it was a privilege to be introduced to Nombulelo, who worshipped at Holy Cross. She was the mother of Mbuyisa who appeared in newspapers across the world in June 1976 pictured running as he carried an injured boy in his arms. It was a photograph which was to play a significant role in international condemnation of apartheid.

School children in Soweto had been protesting against the enforcement of Afrikaans as the language used in schools. No provision was made for local language in schools and Afrikaans was viewed as the language of the oppressor. That June the children's after-school protest turned uneasy when the police arrived. The young people began throwing stones and the shocking response of the police was to open fire. Thirteen year old Hector Pieterson was fatally wounded and the photograph of him lying across the arms of Mbuyisa with Hector's sister Antoinette running at his side was taken by a journalist, Sam Nzima, who then drove Hector to hospital where he was pronounced dead on arrival.

There is now a memorial to Hector Pieterson at the place where he was shot.

[27] Revelation 21:1-5.

Mbuyisa fled to Nigeria as a result of being hounded by the South African security services, but has not been heard of since 1978. Although it is generally assumed that Mbuyisa is no longer alive, Nombulelo told me of her belief that her son would one day return and she had not lost hope. I understand that Nombulelo died in 2004, and for me the story is one full of 'if onlys'.

Although I did not return to Soweto during my sabbatical, I did go back to the Cape where I had undertaken my placement in 1994. It was deeply significant for me, not only because I returned to St Saviour's Claremont where I had spent my placement but also because I revisited the home of Michelle Walker, the wife of my placement supervisor Mark Walker. Over the years they had remained special friends and I was devastated by the news of Mark's illness and subsequent death in 2015. Unfortunately, I had been unable to visit him in South Africa in the short few months of his terminal illness as it was at the time of my appointment as Bishop of Gloucester when I was finishing my post in London and preparing for consecration. That had been a time of 'if only' and I was glad to face the painful reality of Mark's death by returning to South Africa in the summer of 2019 and be able to speak of him and share memories with Michelle and his family, not least on what would have been Mark's sixty-fifth birthday.

Mark taught me so much about Christ-likeness in his passion for justice and the way he enabled the marginalised of South Africa to find a voice and dignity. If ever there was a person who lived and breathed empowerment it was Mark Walker. I will never forget his ministry, not only in parishes but his subsequent posts with NGOs focused on social and racial justice, compassion and a commitment to building strong communities. The last time I had been with Mark was in 2012 when he took me to visit some of the community projects he was supporting in various townships. Both Mark and Michelle are people who over the years have responded with love and compassion to people's 'if onlys' and brought new things to birth; and yet the words of 'if only' are writ large in their own story.

Throughout my life I will go on speaking my honest 'if onlys' just like Mary and Martha and those stricken with pain and fear and grief. To refrain or filter those words would be to hide from authenticity or deny my identity as a child of God. Yet at the same time I know the truth that it is God in whom I live and move and have my being.[28] I want to be the sheep that is willing to lie down in green pastures and not be wanting, and the sheep that has the courage to dare to trust when walking through the valley of the shadow of death, rather than being shrouded in fear.

> The LORD is my shepherd, I shall not want.
> He makes me lie down in green pastures;
> he leads me beside still waters;
> he restores my soul.
> He leads me in right paths
> for his name's sake.
> Even though I walk through the darkest valley,
> I fear no evil;
> for you are with me (Psalm 23:1-4)

Prayer

> Lord, thou knowest what I want,
> if it be thy will that I have it,
> and if it be not thy will,
> good Lord, do not be displeased,
> for I want nothing which you do not want.

Julian of Norwich, 1342 –c.1416

[28] Acts 17-28, the Apostle Paul quoting Aratus.

NOTES

Chapter 12

FEET AND HEART

Now before the festival of the Passover, Jesus knew that
his hour had come to depart from this world and go to
the Father. Having loved his own who were in the world,
he loved them to the end.

During supper Jesus, knowing that the Father had
given all things into his hands, and that he had come
from God and was going to God, got up from the
table, took off his outer robe, and tied a towel around
himself. Then he poured water into a basin and began
to wash the disciples' feet and to wipe them with the
towel that was tied around him. He came to Simon
Peter, who said to him, 'Lord, are you going to wash my
feet?' Jesus answered, 'You do not know now what I am
doing, but later you will understand.' Peter said to him,
'You will never wash my feet.' Jesus answered, 'Unless I
wash you, you have no share with me.' Simon Peter said
to him, 'Lord, not my feet only but also my hands and
my head!' ...

After he had washed their feet, had put on his robe,
and had returned to the table, he said to them, 'Do you
know what I have done to you? You call me Teacher and
Lord—and you are right, for that is what I am. So if I,
your Lord and Teacher, have washed your feet, you also
ought to wash one another's feet.' (John 13:1-14)

Again and again my own feet have played a meaningful role
in bringing me back to the heart of God, so perhaps it is no
coincidence that my physical feet have always been an issue
for me, or that the painting which struck me so forcibly in

the Encounter chapel in Magdala[29] is focused on the area of the disciples' feet as the woman touched the hem of Jesus' garment.

When I was at school, buying shoes was a major headache. With size 8 feet from about the age of fourteen it was no easy task trying to purchase shoes that conformed to school regulations, and it was nigh on impossible to find shoes that would be deemed fashionable by my peers. It's also true to say that my feet have been a focus of my distrust of myself. My apparent fear of heights is actually about a fear of trusting my own feet on narrow paths or climbs, and that includes twisty steps in churches and cathedrals.

My dislike of ballet as a child was most definitely affected by my self-consciousness around my large feet and poor coordination, and it still makes me smile to read my Grade 1 ballet report when a kind-hearted examiner balanced her criticism of my foot work with her comment 'arms pleasing'. It is indeed my arms which now play the visible role in my conversation, speaking and leading of worship, and yet I know that it is my feet with all their imperfections which frequently remind me of my fragility and flaws and connect me back to my heart.

How easy it is to seemingly express my commitment to Christ in all my activity as a priest and bishop, whilst allowing my attention to my heart to grow cold. This came into sharp relief for the first time many years ago as I reflected on Jesus washing the disciples' feet and imagined myself alongside Peter as he resisted and failed to understand.

It was the slave's job to wash the dusty feet of people residing within a home or being welcomed into a place of hospitality. Never would a teacher kneel before his disciples. And as I imagined myself alongside Peter I felt extremely uptight as Jesus came towards me with water and towel. Like Peter, I've frequently expressed a strong commitment to Christ and in my imaginative prayer I recoiled at the idea of Jesus washing my

[29]   See Introduction pp. 23-24.

feet and it wasn't only to do with the strange upturning of roles and status.

You might relate to this if you have ever been present at foot washing in a church service on Maundy Thursday. In whatever ways this is enacted within different Christian worshipping communities and traditions, what seems to be common to human nature is that people do not like to be taken by surprise but prefer to have had the opportunity to wash and prepare their feet in advance. There is an embarrassment and awkwardness for many of us when it comes to someone else seeing and touching our feet which are frequently kept covered.

In my imaginative meditation on John 13 I tried to distract Jesus in conversation as he cupped his fingers around my feet, feeling the hard skin and misshapen nails. And then in a piercing moment I realised that whilst I was so intensely embarrassed of my feet I was not paying the same attention to my heart which was just as exposed to Jesus' sight as my feet.

Why was I not concerned about the cold and hard places of my heart but only the imperfections of my feet? And if I felt embarrassed about Jesus tending my feet but allowed him to do so, could I recognise the cracks and hard places of my heart and allow Jesus to tend those too?

Jesus' act of foot washing took place at the Passover supper the night before he was put to death, and it was not long before Jesus was arrested in the Garden of Gethsemane and taken off to the house of Caiaphas. It would appear from Mark 14:50 that Peter's feet which had been washed by Christ now desert him and flee, although we are told in verse 54 that Peter follows at a distance. However, what becomes clear is that Peter's feet and heart are severely disconnected. The activity of the commitment to Christ is not yet rooted in the love of Christ.

Jesus had known Peter's heart and the fragility of his commitment and in response to Peter's passionate words that he would follow Jesus and even lay down his life for him, Jesus had correctly predicted that Peter would deny him three times.[30]

Only a few hours after Jesus had washed his feet, Peter is in the high priest's courtyard warming himself by the fire. It's just that it's the wrong fire. He has distanced himself almost unknowingly from the fire of God's love, revealed in Christ's foot washing.[31]

If only as he warmed his feet Peter could have remembered Jesus washing those same feet hours earlier. Perhaps he might have remembered Jesus' love and commitment and perhaps Peter's heart might have directed his feet, and he might not have denied Christ.

Perhaps Peter might even have remembered that recent time when rather than Jesus kneeling at *Peter's* feet, Peter had fallen at *Jesus'* feet. They had been at the top of the mountain and Jesus had been transfigured and Peter, James and John had heard God's voice saying, 'This is my Son, the Beloved; with him I am well pleased; listen to him.'[32]

Now, as Peter warmed his body in that courtyard, he failed to remember and he let his heart grow cold out of fear and uncertainty. He let Jesus down and denied even knowing him.

All this was so different from the woman who extravagantly anointed Jesus' feet with expensive perfumed oil. This too had been at a meal and the feet had been all about love.[33]

The host (Simon the Pharisee) and his guests were critical but Jesus made it clear that the woman had shown great love. The critics had not tended their hearts, but the woman knew her brokenness and her tears were plenty. There was no denying Jesus or fleeing from him. Instead, in her anointing of Jesus' feet the woman's heart yearned for the heart of God.

Only hours after Peter had denied Jesus there comes another scene involving feet. Now it is Jesus' feet being nailed to a cross and as with the woman with the perfume, Jesus' feet are utterly connected to his heart as the nails are driven through his feet.

[30]   John 13:38.
[31]   Mark 14:50-54.
[32]   Matthew 17:5.
[33]   Luke 7: 37-38.

Jesus' heart of love is cruelly pierced. His feet were immoveable and yet they were making the greatest journey of all time. This was a journey of love from death to life, and Jesus' feet and heart were intrinsically connected.

When Jesus had knelt to wash his followers' feet he shattered the norm of how power and value is expressed and perceived in the Kingdom of God, yet ultimately that washing of feet was not about Jesus teaching his disciples about structures and hierarchy. This was Jesus saying something profound about the nature of love, which begins not with the activity symbolised by our feet, but with our heart. Although even that is not quite accurate because it implies that it all begins with self. The truth is that it begins with and in the heart of God. The woman who anointed Jesus in Simon's house knew something of that, and some of the most precious moments in my episcopal ministry have been not only washing the feet of ordinands on their pre-ordination retreat, but also washing the feet of women in prison as I have spoken their name and spoken of God's love.

I remembered all this late one evening a few months ago when I was feeling despondent and frustrated regarding my episcopal leadership. It felt to me as if my recent activity had been somewhat lacking in terms of what I had intended. I was irritated with myself and was reflecting on how I might put things right, but subconsciously my thought processes were very much about the activity of striving in my own strength. It was also an evening when I was aware that one of my feet had been hurting that day due to the pressure on some hard skin so amid my night time despondency I forcefully applied a scraper to my feet. A few moments later the tending of my feet reminded me of my heart. It enabled me to stop my frenzied mental striving and to inwardly sit at God's feet as I consciously offered God my fractured inner thoughts and emotions. Unless my heart is open to be transformed by God's love my feet cannot follow in the way. I am reminded of the Prayer of Preparation in the service of Holy Communion:

Almighty God, to whom all hearts are open, all desires
known,
and from whom no secrets are hidden:
cleanse the thoughts of our hearts by the inspiration of
your Holy Spirit,
that we may perfectly love you, and worthily magnify
your holy name;
through Christ our Lord. Amen.[34]

Peter discovered the truths contained in this prayer, and in my
own fallibility I am grateful that in Peter we see someone who
was open to the transforming love of Christ and who did not let
his brokenness have the final word.

After that fire in the courtyard of the high priest there came
another fire, this time on a beach. Jesus is risen from the dead
and comes to be with his disciples at breakfast.[35]

When the risen Christ appears on the shore Peter's feet can't
wait to carry him to Jesus. Following his previous triplicate denial
of Jesus, Peter now declares his love for Christ three times, and
it is now that Jesus says, 'Feed my sheep'. Peter is to be a servant
and a shepherd. He is to wash feet and feed sheep. Jesus has
seen Peter's full potential and it is on Peter that Christ will build
his Church.

Here is Peter's heart in right relationship with Christ as he
begins to discover who he truly is. Peter's activity as a follower
of Christ will now grow from this place of love as his heart
continues to be shaped and transformed by the heart of God.

On my sabbatical visit to Galilee I read this encounter
between Jesus and Peter as told by John.[36] Guy and I were
standing with our feet in the water by the Franciscan Church of
the Primacy of Saint Peter at Tabgah, traditionally regarded as
the place where this beach conversation took place.

After we had been in the water we had gravel in our toes and

---

[34] Church of England *Common Worship*, Order for Holy Communion Prayer
of Preparation, © Archbishops' Council.
[35] John 21:4-17.
[36] John 21.

subsequently stones in our shoes so we sat down to deal with our feet. In an instant that pragmatic act became a holy moment as I reflected once more on the desire of God to go on transforming my heart.

Whilst I find my feet awkward and unsightly and don't entirely trust them, I continue to hope and pray that all of this will remind me of my heart so that I might better tend Christ's sheep:

> ...Be of the same mind, having the same love, being in
> full accord and of one mind. Do nothing from selfish
> ambition or conceit, but in humility regard others as
> better than yourselves. Let each of you look not to your
> own interests, but to the interests of others. Let the same
> mind be in you that was in Christ Jesus,
> who, though he was in the form of God,
> did not regard equality with God
> as something to be exploited,
> but emptied himself,
> taking the form of a slave,
> being born in human likeness.
> And being found in human form,
> he humbled himself
> and became obedient to the point of death—
> even death on a cross. (Philippians 2:2-8)

One other thing struck me at Tabgah. There are pictures of the visit of Pope Paul VI in 1964, noted by the Roman Catholic Church as the first time since the Apostle Peter that a Pope had visited the Holy Land (the popes being seen as the successors of St Peter). However, as I looked at the photographs from 1964 I immediately thought of Pope Francis who shocked the world in April 2019 by kissing the feet of the South Sudanese leaders as he implored them to stay in a place of peace.

The leaders who had previously been at war with one another had recently signed a peace agreement in anticipation of a government of unity, and had been together at the Vatican for an extraordinary retreat convened jointly by the Archbishop of Canterbury, Justin Welby, and Pope Francis. Not unlike Jesus washing the feet of his disciples the Pope's dramatic act was shocking and awkward for those involved. Not unlike Jesus' dealings with Peter, it was an appeal to the heart.

I am ashamed of my pride, strongly challenged, and full of hope, all at the same time.

Prayer

Take my life and let it be
Consecrated, Lord, to Thee.
Take my moments and my days,
Let them flow in endless praise.
Take my hands and let them move
At the impulse of Thy love.
Take my feet and let them be
Swift and beautiful for Thee.
Take my love, my Lord, I pour
At Thy feet its treasure store.
Take myself and I will be
Ever, only, all for Thee.

(Frances Havergal 1874)

NOTES

Chapter 13

EXPLORING
THE DARK

Now there was a Pharisee named Nicodemus, a leader of the Jews. He came to Jesus by night and said to him, 'Rabbi, we know that you are a teacher who has come from God; for no one can do these signs that you do apart from the presence of God.' Jesus answered him, 'Very truly, I tell you, no one can see the kingdom of God without being born from above.' Nicodemus said to him, 'How can anyone be born after having grown old? Can one enter a second time into the mother's womb and be born?' Jesus answered, 'Very truly, I tell you, no one can enter the kingdom of God without being born of water and Spirit. What is born of the flesh is flesh, and what is born of the Spirit is spirit. Do not be astonished that I said to you, "You must be born from above." The wind blows where it chooses, and you hear the sound of it, but you do not know where it comes from or where it goes. So it is with everyone who is born of the Spirit.' (John 3:1-8)

As a bishop in the Church of England it is an immense joy and privilege to confirm young people and adults as they publicly say 'yes' to following Christ.

At the end of the confirmation service each candidate is presented with a candle lit from the Easter candle, and before the service I remind the candidates that when they experience the sadness and pain of life (and many already have), Christ's light, love and hope cannot be extinguished. However, I am also aware that as we send the candidates out to 'shine as a light in the world to the glory of God' in their everyday lives, those candles in their hands are symbolic of something far richer than the over simplified imagery of equating darkness with bad and light with good.

Nicodemus visited Jesus in the dark of night. Presumably the darkness allowed him to go there secretly, after all he was part of the Jewish authority who were opposed to Jesus. It is also true that it is often in the dark of the night-time when questions emerge, and open, vulnerable and discursive conversation take place. I can certainly relate to that when I look back at numerous night-time conversations sitting with individual friends or groups. Encounters in and with the dark take many forms and it is interesting that Jesus' words to Nicodemus about seeing the kingdom of God and being born again implicitly reference the darkness of the womb.

When I give each confirmation candidate their candle I am very aware that the darkness of life is multifaceted.

Sometimes darkness is about evil such as the darkness of hatred, injustice and oppression. It is a darkness which destroys and consumes and prevents life and growth, whether it be something such as human abuse hidden and secret, or the evil of apartheid or the slaughter of genocide – but these are only a few examples of the seemingly overwhelming darkness in which we long for the light.

During my stay in a township in South Africa in 1996 I remember the revelation of reciting the psalms at morning and evening prayer within a community that knew about the darkness of evil. There was no hesitation in speaking the verses that are sometimes marked as optional in the liturgies of the Church of England. If you have seen your children slaughtered or neighbours necklaced with burning tyres, or if you are treated as less human and valuable than fellow human beings who have a different colour skin then why would you recoil from vocalizing words such as, 'O that you would kill the wicked, O God ...' [37] In a place surrounded by the darkness

[37]   Psalm 139:19.

of evil and despair there is a yearning for the light as we try desperately to cling on to the truth that the light of Christ will always be stronger than the darkness which will never overcome the light:

> In the beginning was the Word, and the Word was with God, and the Word was God. He was in the beginning with God. All things came into being through him, and without him not one thing came into being. What has come into being in him was life, and the life was the light of all people. The light shines in the darkness, and the darkness did not overcome it. (John 1:1-5)

The mystery and the wonder of those words strike me year after year at carol services, particularly when it is dark except for the flickering of candlelight.

Jesus' response to Nicodemus is a reminder that as well as the darkness of evil, there is also a darkness which gives birth to life. This is present in the very opening verses of the Bible as we hear God's overarching story of rescue and restoration beginning in a place of darkness. God breathed life into the darkness and continues to do so.[38]

As Jesus speaks to Nicodemus of new life and being born of the Spirit, we are reminded that the tiny embryo in the womb or the seed in the ground are both about the beginning of life growing in the dark, taking shape, being intricately formed and destined for the light.

Sometimes it seems that the darkness of evil can be transformed into this darkness of life. I thought about this on my sabbatical time in South Africa as I looked back to the amazing work and witness of both Archbishop Desmond Tutu and Nelson Mandela in the 1990s and remembered a visit some years later to Mandela's tiny cell on Robben Island where he was imprisoned for eighteen years.

I think too of a project in Bosnia entitled '*Snaga Žene*'

---

[38] Genesis 1:1-4.

(translated as the 'Strength of a Woman'). In chapter 5 of this book I mentioned my visit in 2019. As well as the dreadful massacre of Muslim men and boys in Srebrenica in July 1995, more than 20,000 women across Bosnia suffered rape and sexual violence and many still live alongside their perpetrators.

At the 'Strength of a Woman' project we sat in a small room hearing the story of how some of the women decided to return to Srebrenica after their expulsion and the ethnic cleansing. This caused great concern among professionals who had been trying to support the women, and when they tracked them down in Srebrenica there was a concern for their safety. However, the reply from the women who had returned was that their oppressors had already killed them inside so there was nothing else that could harm them. Yet gradually in a place of loss, death and alienation the women slowly found themselves discovering new life and healing when they began to grow roses, and in time other plants and aromatic herbs planted in the rich dark soil – feeding their senses with beauty. Over the years they have become ambassadors for transformation.

There is something mysteriously powerful here about the truth that crucifixion dwells with resurrection and every Easter morning I am struck afresh by the event of the women going to the tomb where Jesus' body had been placed. These too are women with aromatic herbs.

They went in the early hours of the day as the night darkness lifted, although that was not true of their interior landscape dark with the pain of tragedy and grief. They had been at the scene of the crucifixion and they had witnessed the unspeakable agony of their friend stretched out to die on a cross.[39] It had been a time of intense inner darkness mirroring the physical manifestation of darkness which covered the land as the sun's light failed.[40]

Because it was the eve of the Sabbath there had been no time for a proper burial but once the Sabbath is over the

[39] Mark 15:29-41.
[40] Luke 23:44-45a.

women approach the tomb carrying the necessary spices to embalm Jesus' body. No doubt they also carried many thoughts and emotions. The pain of loss and fractured dreams, the pain of injustice, anger and helplessness. In that present moment of unfamiliar experience I assume that the women gripped the spices they were carrying and clung on to the physical task they were about to undertake – something tangible amid their pain and fear of a tumultuous and unknown future. Yet not for the first time in their adventure with Jesus, the women are confronted with the unexpected. The stone has been moved from the entrance to the tomb. I imagine that there is a sense of disorientation, bewilderment and growing anxiety. Should they run or hide, or should they linger for a while outside the entrance, or instead should they dare to venture into the tomb?

In the account in Luke's gospel we are told that the women went in.[41] It sounds so simple and yet it must have taken courage. I am aware in my own life that when I am fearful or anxious I often want to hold back, to linger on the edges, sometimes clinging to the anxiety rather than immediately entering into the issues.

In my story and in my pastoral encounters with people I have been aware of how often pain brings us to a place of darkness and like tiny insects in the night air we collide disastrously with closed windows as we frantically seek a source of artificial light to flee the darkness.

What first struck me many years ago is that it is only when the women dared to enter the darkness that they encountered the dazzling light of the two angels and began to discover the truth of resurrection.

I remember once sharing these thoughts with Anna Poulson in a paediatric ward. Anna and her husband are both priests and I had the privilege of getting to know them during my time as Archdeacon of Northolt.

When Mark and Anna discovered that the baby they were

41 Luke 24:1–7.

expecting had a rare syndrome, they dared to go into the darkness of the pain. After Lydia was born I had the privilege of baptising her, fully knowing that her life on this earth would be short. It was extremely moving to lead her funeral and burial only a few years later.

In Mark and Anna I encountered a courage to go deep into the darkness and to discover that their precious child offered them new treasure in the upside down kingdom of God. Lydia was a little girl who in her utter dependence and frailty invited them to live one day at a time and not to take life for granted. Lydia was a child who was accepting of all and whose presence was serene and gracious as she challenged all that the world so often peddles regarding strength and beauty.

At Lydia's baptism her candle was lit by the children of a mother who had ended her own life around the time Lydia had been admitted to hospital following her first major fit. The lighting of the wick of that candle was almost defiant as in the agonising pain and darkness there was an acknowledgement that the darkness would never have the final word.

At Lydia's funeral people were confronted with a brightly adorned coffin covered in paint and glue which children and families at the local hospice had participated in creating. The glorious construction reflected the mystery of discovering that sometimes the depths of God's love and grace are sharply tangible in encounters with people who have experienced great pain and who have entered into the mess and darkness of crucifixion and inexplicably discovered the heart of the Easter tomb.

I know that sometimes I can be paralysed by the darkness or run in search of light rather than daring to have the courage to enter the darkness of the tomb within, yet it's only there at its heart that I will find the light and discover resurrection.

In all my reflections on the various shades of darkness I have thought too of the mysterious darkness of God's overshadowing which far from being about evil and pain is actually about God's glory and pre-eminence.

In the second chapter of Luke's gospel we encounter the

Angel Gabriel announcing to Mary that she will be the bearer of God's Son, yet Mary's 'yes' was to begin not in a place of brilliant light but in the darkness of being overshadowed by the Most High.[42] The image is of the Holy Spirit creating a place of darkness from which Mary will enter more intimately into the mysteries of the immanent and yet transcendent God.

I am reminded too of Moses who longed to see God's glory, and in anticipation of God's goodness passing before him, God created a dark place for Moses in the cleft of the rock – a dark place so that he could encounter more fully the God who is closer than close and yet Holy and beyond human grasp or understanding.[43]

This overshadowing is a very different darkness from that which is life-diminishing.

So back to those lit candles held by precious and unique candidates at the point of sending out from a service of confirmation. They are a symbol for me of the many paradoxes of our adventure of faith lived amid darkness and light. There will undoubtedly, as with Nicodemus, be times when we have questions about faith which we long to ask in a darkness which is about privacy and intimacy. There will also be the times of loneliness and yearning so often felt acutely in the dark of night as Jesus himself experienced in the Garden of Gethsemane; and life will most certainly bring the darkness of searing pain, separation, death and desolation, so vividly seen in the darkness of Christ's crucifixion. Yet I pray too for the experience of knowing the darkness of the soil bearing the seed and the darkness of the life-giving tomb. This is the life which Jesus was speaking about with Nicodemus. I pray too for God's overshadowing that, along with those confirmation candidates, I might behold God's glory.

---

[42] Luke 1:34-35.
[43] Exodus 33:21-22.

Prayer

and you held me and there were no words
and there was no time and you held me
and there was only wanting and
being held and being filled with wanting
and I was nothing but letting go
and being held
and there were no words and there
needed to be no words
and there was no terror only stillness
and I was wanting nothing and
it was fullness and it was like aching for God
and it was touch and warmth and
darkness and no time and no words and we flowed
and I flowed and I was not empty
and I was given up to the dark and
in the darkness I was not lost
and the wanting was like fullness and I could
hardly hold it and I was held and
you were dark and warm and without time and
without words and you held me

Janet Morley

Chapter 14

THE GARDEN OF ENCOUNTER

Early on the first day of the week, while it was still dark, Mary Magdalene came to the tomb and saw that the stone had been removed from the tomb. So she ran and went to Simon Peter and the other disciple, the one whom Jesus loved, and said to them, 'They have taken the Lord out of the tomb, and we do not know where they have laid him.' Then Peter and the other disciple set out and went towards the tomb. The two were running together, but the other disciple outran Peter and reached the tomb first. ...

But Mary stood weeping outside the tomb. As she wept, she bent over to look into the tomb; and she saw two angels in white, sitting where the body of Jesus had been lying, one at the head and the other at the feet. They said to her, 'Woman, why are you weeping?' She said to them, 'They have taken away my Lord, and I do not know where they have laid him.' When she had said this, she turned round and saw Jesus standing there, but she did not know that it was Jesus. Jesus said to her, 'Woman, why are you weeping? For whom are you looking?' Supposing him to be the gardener, she said to him, 'Sir, if you have carried him away, tell me where you have laid him, and I will take him away.' 16 Jesus said to her, 'Mary!' She turned and said to him in Hebrew, 'Rabbouni!' (which means Teacher). (John 20:1-4; 11-16)

In this early morning encounter in a garden, I love the fact that through her tears Mary mistakes the risen Jesus for the gardener. There is something beautifully accurate in her mis-identity. After all God the Son was present from the very beginning of time, participating in creation:

> He is the image of the invisible God, the firstborn of all creation; for in him all things in heaven and on earth were created, things visible and invisible, whether thrones or dominions or rulers or powers—all things have been created through him and for him. He himself is before all things, and in him all things hold together.

Here is the Son of God revealed as co-creator with God the Father and God the Holy Spirit, bringing all things into being. Being seen as a gardener could be perceived as quite apt.

Gardens and green spaces so often seem to connect with the inner space within me, and when I left school I chose Reading University not only for the specialist course but also for its green campus set around a lake which became a place for personal reflection. During all my different chapters in London much of my leisure time involved long solitary and reflective walks through London's parks. These were also my place of choice for meeting friends and engaging in deep conversation. Indeed when I was a curate our Monday morning clergy staff meetings invariably took place on Hampstead Heath. We would review the past week and look to the future as we walked and talked.

Now on rest days in the Diocese of Gloucester I enjoy not only the varied open spaces of the countryside, but also the many gardens of historic buildings, and Westonbirt Arboretum remains one of my favourite places to be.

There is something for me about intentionally looking and listening beyond what I see and hear on the surface as I allow God to speak to me through the features and terrain of the landscape.

When I became a vicar my garden in Bethnal Green became a cherished gift both in my times of rest and in my times of turbulence. Prior to that time and since leaving home I had lived in flats without even so much as space for a window box, but I soon discovered that clearing ground, removing dead leaves and flowers, planting and watering could all be life-giving and full of metaphor amid times of refreshment or after a funeral or being alongside the dying or the despairing.

During my sabbatical I spent a day re-visiting Broxbourne in Hertfordshire where I had grown up. I went with Gillian, a precious friend whom I first met at the age of eight when her father came to be vicar of Broxbourne parish church.

We began our excursion that day in the garden of the vicarage and a little later found ourselves in the garden of a childhood friend before peering into the garden of the house where I was born. Swings and sheds and trees now appeared so small compared with my memories of those garden objects which had been ships and houses and so much more in our imaginative play as children.

Those back gardens had also been places of experiencing community – penny sales and fun days for friends, and church spring fayres in the vicarage garden – and I realise how for me gardens have continued to be places of experiencing community.

Each summer in Gloucester we have two weeks that are set aside for parties in the beautiful garden at Bishopscourt. It is a great privilege to host different groups of people each day and the gatherings I particularly enjoy are those which bring together a diverse array of people, experiences and stories. I remember two years ago looking across the lawn and seeing a small group made up of a young Girl Guide, the Lord Lieutenant, a mother and her child with special needs, and a young Iranian representing the local charity working with refugees and asylum seekers. Nearby sat three men from the City Farm laughing with a mayor and a woman from the women's centre. It made my heart sing as I observed equally-precious individuals each with a name and a story encountering each other in a garden which had become a space of hospitality, friendship and conversation.

On the day of revisiting our childhood haunts, Gillian and I walked to the nearby park in Hoddesdon where we had spent so many hours in our younger days. We found the area by a stream flanked by large trees where we had created a whole imaginary world around a narrative of good and evil and friendship. Perhaps even as a child, the external flora and fauna was saying something to me about my interior landscape and the call to be 'rooted and grounded' in the soil of God's love and in relationship with those around me.

The metaphor of the garden has continued to be deeply significant for me in my adventure with God, and the garden of my soul is a strong image in my prayer and thinking. I often find myself using garden imagery in pastoral conversations with people as I hear and see what people are living in their own lives. Sometimes it is about naming seasons of planting or clearing or designing a new landscape. Just as with physical gardens not only can our inner gardens experience changes of season but they also require tending. God is present and the invitation is to explore and discover.

I am not surprised that Mary encounters the risen Jesus in a garden because throughout the overarching story in scripture of God's relationship with the world, gardens have been places of encounter in the narrative of our human being and becoming.

On the opening pages of the Bible we read the narratives of creation and hear of the Garden of Eden, a beautiful place watered by flowing streams. Adam and Eve are to tend it and enjoy it as they live in perfect relationship with God.[44] In the third chapter of Genesis we are presented with a beautiful picture of God walking in the garden in the cool of the evening, and I imagine the golden evening sun and dappled dancing shadows of leafy trees and the delicate evening fragrance of flowers. Yet the harmony is short-lived as Adam and Eve action the first 'no' to God's love and authority, and the garden of freedom and wellbeing becomes a place of fearful hiding[45].

The first garden dwellers' rejection of God's loving authority reveals the pain of alienation: person from person, person from God, person from creation, and so it is that creation's groaning

[44]   Genesis 2:8-10.
[45]   Genesis 3:1-7.

begins and continues.[46] But as the pain of broken relationship fractures the world, God does not abandon it and God goes on to tread in other gardens.

When Jesus has grown to adulthood and has undertaken his ministry of proclaiming and revealing the Kingdom of God, there comes the garden of his arrest: The Garden of Gethsemane. Now not the beautiful and serene cool of the evening, but rather some ugly and turbulent hours of darkness. God the Son, fully God yet fully human, cries out to God the Father in a place of turmoil, and yet unlike the Garden of Eden, Gethsemane is a garden of 'yes' to God.

Then comes the garden of burial. After Jesus' tortuous death his body is placed in a garden where Joseph of Arimathea owned a new sepulchre, hewn out of rock,[47] and so it is that three days later, Mary Magdalene stands weeping in the garden when she realises that Jesus' body has gone.

Pilgrims who visit Jerusalem today are faced with two very different sites each laying claim to be the location of the tomb where Jesus was buried. Personally I found my visit to the Garden of the Empty Tomb in 2015 far more evocative than my visit to the crowded site of the Holy Sepulchre.

Guy and I were with a group who visited the garden on a cold morning in January. There was snow on the ground and our footprints were the first of the day. I had experienced a night of broken sleep, although probably nothing compared to those first female followers of Jesus after they had witnessed his death and as they planned their early morning visit to the tomb.

For me, the night had been disturbed by the prospect of change far less dramatic but still involving uncertainty and unexpected change. The evening before I had received a phone call from London informing me that I had been shortlisted to be a candidate for the interviews to appoint the next Bishop of Gloucester. It was something of a surprise as I had not

---

46 Romans 8:19-23.
47 John 19:41.

known I was on the long-list and the call threw me into a place of internal displacement. The city of Gloucester and the surrounding diocese were unknown to me and I experienced intense surges of adrenaline, fuelled both by excitement and fear. My immediate answer had been that I would reflect on it further when I returned to England, and in the meantime I requested the paperwork.

It was with all that in my heart and mind that I stepped into the quiet snow-covered garden and the space thought by many to be the tomb which held Christ's body.

I'm not sure why or how but a few of us began to sing spontaneously. A few days earlier we had discovered that within our group we had singers of each vocal range and we were able to break into harmony very easily.

The acoustic in the tomb-space was spine-tingling and somehow in that expression of song I heard the call of the risen and ascended Christ to explore this next part of the adventure, knowing that whatever lay ahead in the short term, nothing could undo the unchanging life and hope of resurrection.

In 1998 during my 30-day Ignatian guided retreat I spent a little time reading something of the story of Teresa of Avila, the Spanish sixteenth-century mystic,[48] and was struck by the resonances with my own discoveries regarding the garden of the soul, particularly her reflections around watering. Teresa talks about how at first we make great effort as we draw water from a well and heave it about. However, when the stream appears in the garden, something new takes place as God runs through our lives and waters our soul. It's a picture of moving from a place of striving to a place of repose and it resonates with what I have discovered and yet am so slow to learn. There is a constant temptation to be a water-heaver rather than a stream tender.

In July 2015, several months after that visit to the Garden of the Empty Tomb, I stood alongside Sarah Mullally in

---

[48] *The Life of Saint Teresa of Avila* by herself, translated by J. M.Cohen (Penguin Books, 1957).

Canterbury Cathedral as we were consecrated Bishops in the
Church of God. It was on the Feast Day of Mary Magdalene.

Song

Now the green blade rises from the buried grain,
Wheat that in the dark earth many years has lain;
Love lives again, that with the dead has been:
Love is come again, like wheat that springs up green.

In the grave they laid Him, Love Whom we had slain,
Thinking that He'd never wake to life again,
Laid in the earth like grain that sleeps unseen:
Love is come again, like wheat that springs up green.

Up He sprang at Easter, like the risen grain,
He that for three days in the grave had lain;
Up from the dead my risen Lord is seen:
Love is come again, like wheat that springs up green.

When our hearts are saddened, grieving or in pain,
By Your touch You call us back to life again;
Fields of our hearts that dead and bare have been:
Love is come again, like wheat that springs up green.

John MacLeod Campbell Crum (1872-1958)

NOTES

Chapter 15

THE ROAD TO EMMAUS

Now on that same day two of them were going to a village called Emmaus, about seven miles from Jerusalem, and talking with each other about all these things that had happened. While they were talking and discussing, Jesus himself came near and went with them, but their eyes were kept from recognizing him. And he said to them, 'What are you discussing with each other while you walk along?' They stood still, looking sad. Then one of them, whose name was Cleopas, answered him, 'Are you the only stranger in Jerusalem who does not know the things that have taken place there in these days?' He asked them, 'What things?' They replied, 'The things about Jesus of Nazareth, who was a prophet mighty in deed and word before God and all the people, and how our chief priests and leaders handed him over to be condemned to death and crucified him. But we had hoped that he was the one to redeem Israel. Yes, and besides all this, it is now the third day since these things took place. Moreover, some women of our group astounded us. They were at the tomb early this morning, and when they did not find his body there, they came back and told us that they had indeed seen a vision of angels who said that he was alive. Some of those who were with us went to the tomb and found it just as the women had said; but they did not see him.' Then he said to them, 'Oh, how foolish you are, and how slow of heart to believe all that the prophets have declared! Was it not necessary that the Messiah should suffer these things and then enter into his glory?' Then beginning with Moses and all the prophets, he interpreted to them the things about himself in all the scriptures.

As they came near the village to which they were going, he walked ahead as if he were going on. But they urged him strongly, saying, 'Stay with us, because it is almost evening and the day is now nearly over.' So he went in to stay with them. When he was at the table with them, he took bread, blessed and broke it, and gave it to them. Then their eyes were opened, and they recognised him; and he vanished from their sight. They said to each other, 'Were not our hearts burning within us while he was talking to us on the road, while he was opening the scriptures to us?' That same hour they got up and returned to Jerusalem; and they found the eleven and their companions gathered together. They were saying, 'The Lord has risen indeed, and he has appeared to Simon!' Then they told what had happened on the road, and how he had been made known to them in the breaking of the bread. (Luke 24:13-35)

As I come to the final chapter of this book, I look back on my life so far with gratitude for all those who have walked with me at different points in my life. When I set out to write this book it was not intended as a biography in which everyone significant in my life would get a mention, yet as I have written it I have become acutely aware of all the people I have not named and yet who have taught me so much in a place of encounter, and where Jesus has drawn near but has not always been immediately recognised.

During the weeks of my sabbatical I reconnected with many of those people and the majority of those encounters took place around food, whether in cafes and restaurants or in people's homes. This included the breaking of bread of many different kinds across the world. For example, sitting on a park bench in

England sharing sandwiches with a childhood friend; putting sausages into locally baked baguette on a French hillside with cousins, aunts and uncles; dipping freshly baked bread into hummus in Nazareth; and dipping local rusks into breakfast coffee in South Africa.

For some reason I am reminded of my sister's amazing patchwork quilts. I remember some of the first ones she created many years ago – exquisite works of art involving small pieces of fabric intricately connected together in beautiful shapes. I remember my delight at a jacket she made for me in my first year at university. So many of the fabric pieces held a story as they were taken from garments of different chapters of life reflecting relationship and love. There was my mother's wedding dress, a child's cotton dress made for me by my grandmother and material from clothes made for members of the family when babies. Perhaps if I had looked long enough and invited the stories from the mouths of others, I might have understood some things in fresh ways – not unlike the day when my brother and sister and I were with my parents looking at old photographs.[49]

Going back to those disciples on the road, I realise that I have been doing theology on the journey – I have seen and recognised new things as I have read and talked about Scripture and as the Holy Spirit has been at work constantly bringing me to new places of recognition and sometimes enabling me to live the painful process of undoing my strongly held convictions.

This mysterious walk on the road to Emmaus seems to be much about talking and discussing: the disciples with one another and then with Jesus, the disciples telling of what the women had said, and of course Jesus' own verbal interpretation of the Scriptures. Yet as I dwell in this passage, it is the listening which strikes me most strongly – and interestingly it is Jesus who seems to listen first. This listening of Christ is then followed by his robust and compassionate response to the companions on the road and I am once again challenged by our eagerness to so often offload everything in prayer that verbalises our thoughts,

---

[49]   See Chapter 10.

emotions, longings and fears but our failure to wait in silence to have 'the mind of Christ',[50] so that, in the words of St Richard of Chichester[51] we might see Christ 'more clearly, love more dearly and follow more nearly'.

The disciples had heard much but had not seen. The women had seen but somehow their talking about it to the other disciples was not enough. The mysterious revelation of the truth comes in an action – the breaking of the bread – presumably accompanied by a Jewish prayer of blessing as Jesus unexpectedly takes the place of host not guest.

For me, recognising the presence of Christ has often come after the talking, the discussing or the reading. It has been in those moments of silence and of revelation as I have seen something which suddenly connects back to words of scripture I have heard, read or discussed.

In the opening pages of this book I spoke of my thirty-day Ignatian retreat – days of silence in which I discovered deep truths about myself and God as I spent time dwelling in scripture and prayer.

As I reflect on those disciples recognising Christ I am reminded of a day on that retreat when I was contemplating another time when disciples recognised Christ in a new way. I was reading chapter 17 of Matthew's gospel and reflecting on the Transfiguration of Christ when his face *'shone like the sun and his clothes became as dazzling as light'*. It was a beautiful autumnal morning and I had taken my coffee and breakfast outside and as I sat on the bench eating fresh bread made by the sisters in the retreat house, the sunlight fell on the dewy grass in such a way that it was as if someone had taken handfuls of tiny diamonds and scattered them across the lawn. Somehow in that moment, as with Peter at the transfiguration, I encountered the majesty of my creator and was overwhelmed by a sense of intimacy with Christ. For a few moments I stopped eating and beheld the majesty of God – but my overwhelming sense of wholeness was

---

[50] Philippians 2:5.
[51] St Richard of Chichester (1197 – 1253).

quickly intercepted by a sharp inner pain as I realised that like Peter I would fail to 'hold on' to this moment so that it would change me forever. Yet I longed to remember.

I wonder how well those companions on the road went on to remember the truth of the encounter with Jesus Christ at Emmaus.

It has taken me a long time to finish this final chapter since returning to the rhythm of ministry following my sabbatical, and yet it is so poignant now to be doing so during the time of national 'lockdown' amid the COVID-19 outbreak of 2020.

It is a time when people are living behind closed doors, either in households or alone and it is not a time of physically walking side by side or inviting people into our homes to share food. Yet it is a time of trying to make sense of the bewildering present, and a time to remember as we hold fast to all that is constant in the love and promises of God as we keep walking and reflecting.

In Luke's beautiful telling of the walk to Emmaus we are told that after they recognise Jesus in the breaking of the bread, the companions get up and return to Jerusalem where they find the eleven and their companions gathered together. Then in chapter 20 of John's gospel[52] we are told of an encounter that first Easter evening in Jerusalem between the disciples and Jesus, who comes and stands among them and says, 'Peace be with you.' The disciples are gathered behind locked doors 'for fear of the Jews', and it is my prayer during this time of 'lockdown' that as households and individuals are isolated behind locked doors, people might know the presence of Christ speaking words of peace. I pray that too for prisons and hospitals and so many places where people of all ages are in a place of fear and turbulence and unknowing. I pray peace too for homes where there is an increase in violence and anger and turbulence.

It is healing for me now to look back and remember that garden of jewelled grass more than twenty years ago.

As I sat with my breakfast bread in that garden, I was reminded of the special landmarks the People of Israel established as they

---

[52] John 20:19-21.

journeyed – physical heaps of stones to mark special places where they experienced God. I recalled particularly the story in the final chapter of Joshua in which Joshua confronts the people and asks them 'whom they choose to serve this day' – Yahweh or the gods of their ancestors?[53] The people call to remembrance the God who brought them out of Egypt and they pledge to serve Yahweh. Joshua then sets a large stone at Shechem as a witness to the covenant between the people and God.

So it was that in that garden on retreat I chose a stone as witness to my experience of God and my deep desire to serve him. It's my 'transfiguration stone' and it sits in front of me on my desk. It is also a 'transformation stone' to remind me, as I commented in Chapter 6, that God has given me a new heart of *flesh* and removed my heart of *stone*.

The stone in front of me is currently a memory of recognising Christ's presence in a place of eating bread in solitude – so pertinent at this time of the COVID-19 pandemic, not least when worshipping communities cannot come together as the Body of Christ to be fed by God in bread and wine.

I love the fact that Emmaus is an unknown place. And right now it feels as if I am encouraging people to keep walking, but I truly don't know the destination of the next season. For me that describes my experience in life of walking purposefully but never truly knowing where I will end up. If ever there was a time for doing theological reflection it is now.

I am fortunate in this time of viral pandemic to be alongside Guy who has been my beloved companion for fourteen years. I give thanks for the walks we have shared, sometimes talking but often walking in silence through beautiful scenery, looking and listening. It is often in those times when I begin to make sense of things, and indeed pray and let Scripture be at work within me. When I have a sermon to write I will often reflect on the Scripture as I walk, and it is often in those times that I sense the Holy Spirit illuminating key messages and provoking recognition.

---

[53] Joshua 24:14 – 15:26.

The final reflective song of this book is one that Guy and I had at our wedding, then at my consecration in Canterbury Cathedral. To me, it speaks of mutual encounter and relationship in joy and in pain and in which Christ is present and made known

In this time of worldwide pandemic, I am acutely aware of wanting to hold the Christ light for people in the night-time of their fear. I cannot hold out my physical hand, but it is a time of reaching out a hand across virtual networks, telephone and written cards and letters.

It is a time of weeping with those who weep and rejoicing with those who rejoice. It is a time of sharing in joy and sorrow 'till we've seen this journey through'.

And then, when this season is over, there will come another, and the journeys of encounter will continue until my life's end, and my words to Jesus, like those of the friends on the road to Emmaus are 'stay with me' or rather 'stay with us' because this is about encounters with Jesus Christ in a place of relationship with people and all of creation.

Prayer: 'The Servant Song'

Brother, sister, let me serve you,
let me be as Christ to you;
pray that I may have the grace to
let you be my servant too.
We are pilgrims on a journey,
and companions on the road;
we are here to help each other
walk the mile and bear the load.
I will hold the Christ-light for you
in the night-time of your fear;
I will hold my hand out to you,
speak the peace you long to hear.
I will weep when you are weeping;
when you laugh I'll laugh with you;
I will share your joy and sorrow
till we've seen this journey through.

When we sing to God in heaven
we shall find such harmony,
born of all we've known together
of Christ's love and agony.
Brother, sister, let me serve you,
let me be as Christ to you;
pray that I may have the grace to
let you be my servant too.

Words: Richard A. M. Gillard, 1977

NOTES

ACKNOWLEDGEMENTS

Thanks are due to the following for permission to quote copyright material:

'Will You Come and Follow Me?' (The Summons). Words: John L. Bell (b. 1949) and Graham Maule (1958 - 2019). Copyright © 1987 WGRG, c/o Iona Community, Glasgow, Scotland. reproduced by permission: www.wildgoose.scot.

'Take This Moment'. Words: John L. Bell (b. 1949) and Graham Maule (1958 – 2019). Copyright © 1989, 2000 WGRG, c/o Iona Community, Glasgow, Scotland, Reproduced by permission: www.wildgoose.scot.

'Methodist Covenant Prayer' taken from the Methodist Worship Book © 1999 Trustees for Methodist Church Purposes. Used with permission.

Oxford University Press for permission to reproduce 'Now the green blade rises' by John MacLeod Campbell Crum.

SPCK for permission to reproduce the poem 'And you held me', taken from *All Desires Known* by Janet Morley.

'The Servant Song' by Richard Gillard; issued under license from Universal Music Publishing Int. Ltd on behalf of Universal Music, Brentwood Benson Publ. and Capitol Christian Music group.

NOTES

NOTES

NOTES